PUERTO RICANS

VALUE ORIENTATIONS AND ACHIEVEMENT POTENTIAL

DIEGO L. COLÓN

IUNIVERSE, INC.
NEW YORK BLOOMINGTON

Puerto Ricans
Value Orientations and Achievement Potential

iUniverse books may be ordered through booksellers or by contacting:

iUniverse
1663 Liberty Drive
Bloomington, IN 47403
www.iuniverse.com
1-800-Authors (1-800-288-4677)

Because of the dynamic nature of the Internet, any Web addresses or links contained in this book may have changed since publication and may no longer be valid.

ISBN: 978-1-4502-0435-4 (sc)
ISBN: 978-1-4502-0433-0 (dj)
ISBN: 978-1-4502-0434-7 (ebk)

Printed in the United States of America

iUniverse rev. date: 2/19/2010

CONTENTS

LIST OF TABLES

PREFACE

As I, retrospectively, take a look to my long-term teaching, administering, and research career within Puerto Rico and New York City, I feel a reassurance in the significant importance that the main topics of my research *value orientations and achievement potential modes* play in the educational and personal growth and development of every student. In general, the value orientations of a given culture reflect that group's assumptions concerning their view of the universe, people's relation to the universe, consensus over general philosophy and objectives of the society, family solidarity and relations to others, individual development, definition of work, definition of religion and moral conduct (Miller 1972), while achievement potential is represented in the two specific modes of achievement via conformance and via independence.

Observing differences in the value orientations and achievement modalities of Puerto Rican students while teaching and doing research in both settings of Puerto Rico and New York City, I felt strongly motivated in pursuing research in the value orientations and achievement potential modalities of Puerto Rican students born and reared in Puerto Rico and in New York City. As I completed this piece of research, requests for data contained within it have been continuously received mainly from doctoral students and academicians. Thus, my realization of the significant importance of value orientations and achievement potential modes in the personal and educational development of every student and my motivation in publishing the entire doctoral dissertation emerged. This publication of the dissertation *Value Orientations and Achievement Potential Modes of Island and Mainland Puerto Rican College Students* is primarily geared, but not limited, to the specific audience of students of graduate studies and academicians within the education, social sciences, and ethnic studies disciplines, among others. It has been my empirical observation throughout my teaching and research career that assessing, creating/recreating/transcreating, and adopting value orientations and achievement potential modalities and integrating them within the curricula will raise academic performance, invigorate self-worth and self-efficacy of the student within the school systems of Puerto Rico and the United States.

ACKNOWLEDGMENTS

This book is a product, through the years, of the guidance and support of my doctoral dissertation committee. The inspiration, assistance, and support given to me by Dr. Antonio Simoes, chairperson, is deeply appreciated.

To Dr. Martin Deutsch, I would like to express my appreciation for his constructive guidance and support.

To Dr. Robert Malgady, *mi amigo*, there is no word to express my gratitude to your dedication, sensitivity, and understanding of what it took me to undertake this research. *Gracias*, Bob, for all your assistance, especially in the treatment and analysis of the data.

The data collection was possible, thanks to the enthusiastic cooperation of several colleagues headed by Professors Manuel Febres and Luis Muñoz.

I want to thank all the Puerto Rican students (islanders and mainlanders) who participated in this study for their willingness and kindness in making it possible.

I am deeply grateful to Dr. Richard Fox, Mr. José Bermudez, and Mr. Eduardo Gil of Kingsborough Community College for their invaluable cooperation in coding and computing the data.

Finally, by no means least, I am grateful to my friends Dr. Barbara Sjostrom, Dr. Lilian Sánchez, Dr. Paul Proctor, Ms. Gloria Ríos, and Ms. Evelyn Santiago.

A mis padres Natalio Colón y Trinidad Calderón que inventaron mi vida. A Rosita y nuestra prole Yahaira, Isamar, Diego Juan y Mónica que recrearán mi vida, esta obra es dedicada.

INTRODUCTION

VALUE ORIENTATIONS AND ACHIEVEMENT POTENTIAL MODES OF ISLAND AND MAINLAND PUERTO RICAN STUDENTS

The Puerto Rican mass migration from the 1920s through the 2000s has resulted in four, and in some cases five, generations of Puerto Ricans born and reared on the United States mainland. These generations are most frequently exposed to their parents' and ethnic community's cultural norms during their upbringing. At the same time, they are socialized from an early age into the cultural norms of the United States through mass media, schools, and other institutions. These two different sociocultural systems create a bicultural life situation that influences the achievement value orientations of Puerto Rican students. While achievement motivation is a psychological characteristic that provides an internal impetus to excel, achievement values are culturally determined orientations that delineate the areas in which such excellence should or may take place (Rosen 1966, Winterbottom 1966). The low achievement scores that current assessment measures show for Latinos and Puerto Rican college students in United States schools may be attributed to conflict in values and achieving behavior. Merton (1968) emphasizes this principle when he states that what a person learns and knows is determined by the society of which that person is part.

Deutsch (1968) asserts that the favorability or unfavorability of environmental factors influences the development process for all children, regardless of racial or ethnic group. The experiences and subsequent self-concept and world concept of children are determined by the conditions under which they live and grow up. Dissimilarities in the growth processes of children become maximized when their actual life conditions are dissimilar. As a result, attitudes and patterns of behavior and learning, though basically reflecting the larger culture, assume particular and often marked subgroup characteristics. The influence of environmental factors on the intensity of motivation and on the growing child's self-attitudes regarding his own capabilities is significant.

Simoes (1976) holds that knowledge is culturally bound, that awareness of cultural prescription postulates is needed before the application of knowledge is made, that knowledge is schematized as a system that cannot stand on its own and must be applied to a cultural framework. It must be assumed that learning must be analyzed from the point of view of cultural variables and that no learning theory can be applied without the knowledge of the culture.

In his work on human intelligence, Gardner (1983) suggests that there is persuasive evidence for the existence of several human intelligences, that these are relatively independent of one another, and that they can be fashioned and combined in a multiplicity of adaptive ways by individuals and cultures. In this work, Gardner challenges the prevailing notion of a single intelligence and puts forth a different view of human intellectual competencies. Gardner argues that we are all born with the potential to develop a multiplicity of intelligences, most of which have been overlooked in our testing society, and all of which can be drawn upon to make us competent individuals. Ramírez and Price (1976) concluded that contextual conditions are most important in the expression of achievement motivation and that the particular form in which achievement is expressed is determined by the definition that culture gives to it. The findings of Gray (1975) with Mexican Americans support the latter conclusion by confirming that the preferred mode of achievement motivation—achievement for the benefit of self and achievement for the benefit of others—varies depending upon the cultural values that define the achievement setting. In the area of achievement potential and motivation, prevailing assessment measures have paid specific attention to the difference between the motive to achieve and the manner in which this motive is actualized dependent on culturally approved means and ends. However, the achievement motivation literature stresses that achievement depends on a generalized desire to achieve; it does not deal with the issue of whether or not a culture values the appropriate achievement behavior. For instance, initial studies of achievement motivation conducted with middle-class white males showed that high-need achievers valued achievement for self (McClelland, Atkinson, Clark, and Lowell, 1953). In contrast, studies conducted in this area with Japanese Americans and Mexican Americans showed that high-need achievers were more inclined to pursue goals benefiting others, particularly the family. Success for oneself was seen as a sign of excessive immoral egoism (DeVos 1968, Gray 1975). According to Maehr (1974), the desire to achieve is often confounded with the goal to achieve. Therefore, the result that one might exhibit behaviors characteristic of highly motivated persons, only directed to different goals that are acceptable in one culture but not in another, is plausible.

In 1950, Florence Kluckhohn postulated five value dimensions, which grow out of people's effort to solve five basic problems that are imminent in the human situation. Kluckhohn provided a schema to study configurational patterns of value orientations in a particular culture or social stratum. Value orientations are complex, patterned (rank-ordered) principles that give order and direction to human acts and thoughts as these relate to the solution of "common human" problems (Kluckhohn 1950). Five problems were singled out as the crucial ones common to all human groups. These problems were stated in the form of questions. After the questions are the titles used to denote the five value orientations: (1) What is the character of innate human nature? (human nature-orientations). (2) What is the relation of people to nature and supernature? (people-nature orientations). (3) What is the temporal focus of human life? (time orientations). (4) What is the modality of human activity? (activity orientations). (5) What is the modality of people's relationship to others? (relational orientations).

Several studies have been conducted that deal with differences in value orientation across culture (Kluckhohn 1951, Schermerhorn 1970, Simoes, 1971, O'Flannery 1972, Wurzel 1979, Portes 1980, Sjostrom 1983). These researchers contend that the closeness of fit between the immigrant and host societal value orientations is a variable in the rate of acculturation for the immigrant, whereby the closer the fit, the more rapid the acculturation. Most investigation of culture contact assume that acculturation leads to assimilation or integration. This could occur through the absorption of one culture into another, usually the migrant or minority group into the dominant one (Doob 1960, Lieberson 1961, Gordon 1964) or through the development of a new culture, which responds to the needs of both groups and which has characteristics taken from the interacting cultures (Redfield 1936, Humphrey 1943, Pederson 1950, Lieberson 1961, Blane and Yamamoto 1970). In sociology this latter phenomenon is usually referred to as cultural pluralism. Cultural pluralism as Ginorio (1979) defines it is the result of selective retention from the migrant's culture and selective acquisition from the host's culture of those cultural behaviors and values, which are most meaningful to the migrant. However, as Gómez Peña and Foucault assert, racial /ethnic groups, in addition of retaining and selecting cultural behaviors and values as Ginorio states, have used and are using inventive languages to transcreate, to create multicultural behaviors and values generating the dynamics for political and cultural prominence.

CHAPTER 1

THE STUDY

This type of study was of particular need, given the uniqueness of the Puerto Rican immigration as compared to other immigrant groups. Some of the factors that make this group different have been pointed out by Fitzpatrick, Anselmo, and Lopez: (1) the first group to come in large numbers from a different cultural and linguistic background (Spanish speaking) who were, nevertheless, citizens of the United States; (2) the first airborne migration to the United States; (3) the first massive immigration of a group with widespread intermarriage across racial lines; and (4) the first group of Catholic immigrants unaccompanied by their own clergy.

In light of the uniqueness of this immigrant group and these differentiating factors and given the large numbers of individuals of second-generation Puerto Rican background residing in the United States, it is plausible, therefore, in cultural contact situations such as those inherent in the United States and Puerto Rico, that differences between the relational value orientations of mainlander and islander Puerto Ricans may be viewed as indicators of the modality in which their achievement potential is actualized. Although under Kluckhohn's model, Wurzel (1979) and Sjostrom (1983) investigated Puerto Ricans' value orientations and other variables, no empirical study had been conducted that examines value orientations and mode of achievement potential for mainland Puerto Ricans with their island Puerto Rican peers, ascertaining the relationship of the relational value orientations and mode of achievement potential for both groups. The need for such a study is emphasized by Vazquez (1979) when he shows that the process of formal socialization that is transmitted to Puerto Rican students is plagued with value contradictions at two levels: (a) in the instrumental-rational content of those value orientations conceived as basic to social change and (b) in the degree of consistency between corresponding value orientations. Moreover, Gray (1975) highly recommends research in the area of cultural and sex differences in achievement motivation when she states that future investigations are needed to determine whether the differences in mode of achievement revealed in her study might also hold for students in other cultural groups and different age groups. Further recommendations are to study differences in mode of achievement in other countries, such as Mexico and Japan, and compare the results with those for Mexican Americans and Japanese Americans to evaluate the impact of acculturation on mode of achievement.

The basic assumption of this study is that mainland and island schools reinforce a modality to achieve which stresses contrasting achievement values. For example, the value placed on competitive education in United States school seems to contradict the value placed on cooperative and collaborative education in Puerto Rican school. In order to bridge the gap between the school policies and practices of these two different educational systems, in the sense that the school reflects an understanding and acceptance of differences in the values underlying achievement potential, it was imperative to undertake empirical exploration of the relational value orientations and achievement mode differences of islander and mainlander Puerto Rican college students. Knowledge about these two areas facilitate an understanding of the relational value orientations and achievement potential the children bring into the school and any changes undergone as a result of the school's socializing function. The work of educators in multicultural settings of the United States as well as in Puerto Rico, especially in the areas of curriculum and instruction, may be enhanced by a comprehension of the relational value orientations and preferred mode of achievement potential prevalent among multicultural learners in their classes. Data regarding the relationship of relational value orientations and mode of achievement potential may be of importance in ascertaining whether this relationship is in fact a behavior pattern, culturally and or situationally prescribed. Youngsters of Puerto Rican parentage reared on the mainland, as well as native Puerto Rican youngsters of the same age group and comparable socioeconomic background reared on the island, may thus have learned different modes of achievement potential and different relational value orientations.

DEFINITION OF TERMS

For the purpose of this study, the following terms are defined:

OPERATIONAL DEFINITIONS

Relational value orientations refers to the definition of people's relation to others. This orientation has three subdivisions: lineality, collaterality, and individuality. *Lineality* refers to the relational value orientation that calls for a primacy of groups goals. Continuity through time and ordered positional succession is one of the most important goals of the group. *Collaterality* refers to the relational value orientation that calls for a primacy of their goals and welfare of the laterally extended group. Individuality refers to the relational value orientation that calls for a primacy of the individual goals over the goals of specific collateral or lineal groups (Kluckhohn 1961).

Operationally, mainland and island Puerto Ricans' relational value orientations were measured by scores received on the subscale of Kluckhohn value-orientation schedule (KVOS).

Mode of achievement potential refers to the need for achievement via conformance (Ac) and need for achievement via independence (Ai). For the purpose of this study, Ac will be equivalent to the achievement for the benefit of others (toward others), and Ai will be equivalent to achievement for the benefit of self (toward self).

Operationally, mainland and island Puerto Ricans' mode of achievement potential were measured by the scores they obtained on the subscale of the California Psychological Inventory (CPI) (Gough 1957).

Island Puerto Ricans refer to Puerto Ricans who were born and reared in Puerto Rico and had not lived in the continental United States for more than three consecutive months.

Operationally, island Puerto Ricans were selected through the use of a personal data questionnaire (PDQ) devised by the investigator.

Mainland Puerto Ricans refers to Puerto Ricans, who were born and reared in the continental United States, are the progeny of island Puerto Ricans and have not lived in Puerto Rico for more than three consecutive months.

Operationally, mainland Puerto Ricans were selected through the use of the personal data questionnaire (PDQ) devised by the investigator.

Conceptual Definitions

Values: The term refers to core conceptions of the desirable within every individual and society. They serve as standards or criteria to guide not only action but also judgment, choice, and rationalization (Williams 1968).

Value orientations: The term referring to complex but definitely patterned (rank-ordered) principles that give order and direction to the ever-flowing stream of human acts and thoughts as they relate to the solution of "common problems" (F. Kluckhohn 1961).

Acculturation: The term referring to the absorption process of one culture into another, usually the migrant or minority group into the dominant one (Gordon 1964, Doob 1960), or to the development process of a new culture, which responds to the needs of both groups and which has characteristics taken from the interacting cultures (Bland and Yamamoto 1970).

Statement of the Problem

The purpose of this study was to investigate the relationship of the relational value orientations with the mode of achievement potential of mainland and island Puerto Rican college students. Many studies have been conducted that deal with the differences in value orientation across culture (Kluckhohn 1951, Schemerhorn 1970, Simoes 1971, Flannery 1972, Wurzel 1979, Portes 1980, Sjostrom 1983). These researchers contend that the closeness of fit between the immigrant and host societal value orientations is a variable in the rate of acculturation for the immigrant, whereby the closer the fit, the more rapid the acculturation. Most investigators of culture contact assume that acculturation leads to assimilation or integration. This could occur through the absorption of one culture into another, usually the migrant or minority group into the dominant one (Doob 1960, Lieberson 1961, Gordon 1964) or through the development of a new culture that responds to the needs of both groups and that has characteristics taken from the interacting cultures (Redfield 1936, Humphrey 1943, Pederson 1950, Lieberson 1961, Blane and Yamamoto 1970). In sociology this latter phenomenon is usually referred to as cultural pluralism, the result of selective retention from the migrants' culture and selective acquisition from the hosts' culture of those cultural behaviors and values that are most meaningful to the migrant (Ginorio 1979). Although under Kluckhohn's model, Wurzel (1979) and Sjostrom (1983) investigated Puerto Ricans' value orientations and other variables, no empirical study had been conducted that examines value orientations and mode of achievement potential for mainland Puerto Ricans and their island Puerto Rican peers to ascertain the relationship between the relational value orientations and mode of achievement potential for both groups. The achievement motivation literature stresses that achievement depends on a generalized desire to achieve; it does not deal with the issue of whether or not a culture values the appropriate achievement behavior. For instance, initial studies of achievement motivation conducted with middle-class white males showed that high-need achievers valued achievement for self (McClelland, Atkinson, Clark, and Lowell 1953). In contrast, studies conducted in this area with Japanese Americans and Mexican Americans showed that high-need achievers were more inclined to pursue goals benefiting others, particularly the family (DeVos 1968, Gray 1975). According to Maehr (1974), the desire to achieve is often confounded with the goal to achieve. In his work on human intelligence, Gardner (1983) suggests that there is persuasive evidence for the existence of several human intelligences, that these are relatively independent of one another, and that they can be fashioned and combined in a multiplicity of adoptive ways by individuals and cultures. In light of Gardner's proposition of cultural variations in cognitive and achievement potential and given the large number of Puerto Ricans presently residing in the United States, it is plausible, in cultural contact situations such as those inherent in the United States and Puerto Rico, that differences between relational value orientations of mainlander and islander Puerto Ricans may be viewed as indicators of the modality in which their achievement potential is actualized. The further result that Puerto Rican students might exhibit behaviors characteristic of intellectual potential directed to different goals that are acceptable in the Hispanic culture but not in the Anglo-Saxon culture is also plausible.

According to Steiner (1975), Puerto Ricans born and reared in New York consider themselves to be Puerto Rican. To the island-born Puerto Ricans, the New York Puerto Ricans are just other American mainlanders. Yet to a non–Puerto Rican, both the islanders and mainlanders are Puerto Ricans. Despite the degrees of acculturation among the generations of Puerto Ricans, Americans still characterize mainland Puerto Ricans as Hispanics while Puerto Ricans are considered Americans by their Hispanic American cousins. Among the migrations with strong return flows has been that from Puerto Rico. In 1978, the *New York Times* stated that for the first time in American history, a major immigrant group is giving up on the American dream and returning to the homeland (Stockton 1978).

It appears that differences in environmental factors and sociocultural orientations might result in two distinct ethnic groups with similar cultural heritage, one emerging from the migrant parent group and the other from native islanders. In relation to the groups sampled in this study, composed of Puerto Rican college students, the role of schooling takes on vital importance. The socialization processes inherent in the United States institutions, which mainland Puerto Ricans undergo, foster the dominant value orientations of the American society. Public education in the United States, historically, has served the dual function of transmitting knowledge and culture deemed necessary for adult participation with U.S. society. An important role of schooling during this century, consequently, has been that of fostering the acculturation of the diverse immigrant groups whose descendants are being instructed in American values through the school system (Greer 1974, Tyack 1974). As Greer (1974) pointed out, by the beginning of the twentieth century, urban public schools were already part of the "fixed order of things." They were believed to provide a common experience for the diverse children they were to equip with the wherewithal for responsible USA citizenship. Yet the island Puerto Ricans undergo the socialization processes inherent in the Puerto Rican school system. The school systems of New York City and Puerto Rico differ in curriculum goals and content, methodology, course of study, physical plants, equipment, and environment. Brameld (1958) compared mainland schools and Puerto Ricans schools and wrote that a noteworthy difference among others was in the greater centralization of the islandwide system of Puerto Rico as well as in curricula and teaching methods. Gomez Tejera and López Cruz (1970), as well as Seda-Bonilla (1973), pointed out similar differences in island and mainland school systems as indicated by Brameld. Epstein (1970) noted the additional difference between mainland and island school systems of language of instruction . Spanish is seen as the symbol of Puerto Rican nationalism and culture. The impact of this issue on the island's public school system is fully discussed by Epstein. In addition, Christensen (1975) pointed out several differences between island and mainland schools, which showed that the public educational environments were dissimilar in language instruction, curriculum, methodology, and centralization of the school system. Mainland and island schools reinforce a modality to achieve which stresses contrasting values. For example, the value placed on competitive achievement in the United States schools seems to contradict the value placed on cooperative achievement in Puerto Rico schools. In order to bridge the gap between the school policies and practices of these two different educational systems, in the sense that the school reflects an understanding and acceptance of differences in the values underlying achievement potential, it was imperative to undertake empirical exploration of the relational value orientations and achievement modes of islander and mainlander Puerto Rican college students.

In view of the varying cultural ethos within each society and the different educational systems to which mainland and island Puerto Ricans are exposed to, it was expected that these two groups would differ from each other in their relational value-orientation preferences as well as in their mode of achievement potential. Although there is extensive literature on the subject of cross-cultural difference in value orientations as well as achievement motivation, no study of value orientations had examined the relational value orientation and achievement potential modality of mainlander and islander Puerto Ricans. This study attempted to do so by examining both the modality of relating to others (relational value orientations) and the mode of achievement potential (achievement for the benefit of self or achievement for the benefit of others) in these two groups.

SUBPROBLEMS

In light of the fact that the specific problem of this study was to investigate and examine the relationship of the relational value orientations and the mode of achievement potential of Puerto Ricans born and reared in the metropolitan areas of San Juan and New York City, the following are the subproblems:

1. How do Puerto Rican islanders and mainlanders differ in linealistic, collateralistic, and/or individualistic value orientations?

2. How do Puerto Rican islanders and mainlanders differ in mode of achievement potential via conformance (toward others) or via independence (toward self)?

HYPOTHESES

This study is concerned with variation in the modality of mainland and island Puerto Rican students' relationship to others and in the mode of their achievement potential. The rationale behind the following hypotheses is the thesis that achievement potential may vary with regard to relational value orientations of a particular ethnic group.

The main hypotheses tested were as follows:

1. A positive linear relationship exists between relational value orientations and achievement potentials.

   a. A positive linear relationship exists between linealistic and collateralistic value orientations and achievement via conformance (toward others).

b. A positive linear relationship exists between individualistic value orientation and achievement via independence (toward self).

2. A significant difference exists between mainland and island Puerto Rican students' mode of achievement potential

a. Island Puerto Ricans will show stronger need to achieve for others (via conformance) than mainland Puerto Ricans.

b. Mainland Puerto Ricans will show a stronger need to achieve for self (via independence) than island Puerto Ricans.

3. A significant difference exists between mainland and island Puerto Rican students' relational value-orientations

a. Island Puerto Ricans will show stronger preferences for linealistic and collateralistic value-orientations than mainland Puerto Ricans.

b. Mainland Puerto Ricans will show stronger preferences for individualistic value-orientations than island Puerto Ricans.

DELIMITATIONS

This study did not deal with gender differentiation. What qualified the subjects was the fact of being island-born Puerto Rican or mainland-born Puerto Rican in accord with the definition of terms.

In addition, the topic of this research was delimited to focus only on the relational value orientations—one of the five value orientation dimensions postulated by F. Kluckhohn (1950–1958)—and on the mode of achievement potential in order to permit specific treatment and yet have sufficient significance to warrant investigating it.

LIMITATIONS OF THE STUDY

The generalizations drawn from the findings of this investigation are limited to young adults enrolled in college programs at public institutions, not to a cross section of the Puerto Rican population from the island or the mainland.

The scope of the study is limited to an analysis of variations in relational value orientations and mode of achievement potential for second-generation mainland Puerto Rican college students when compared to the island Puerto Rican sample. The study did not include a sample of third-generation mainland Puerto Ricans, which would show intergenerational changes and enhance the historical perspective of this research by showing a point of comparison with early studies on immigrant groups to the United States (e.g., Irish, Dutch, Swedish, German, etc.). The current literature about the acculturation of these groups provides an analysis of three generations within the host society as a general rule. However, for the purposes of this study, such inclusion was not possible since the massive Puerto Rican immigrations to the United States was a mid-century phenomenon, with the largest number having arrived during the decade of the 1950s.

CHAPTER II

ACHIEVEMENT POTENTIAL

Mode of achievement potential refers to the need of achievement via conformance (Ac) and need for achievement via independence (Ai). For the purpose of this study, Ac was equivalent to achievement for the benefits of others (toward others), and Ai was equivalent to achievement for the benefit of self (toward self).

Following the early work on achievement motivation, researchers began to focus on the relationship of achievement and socialization practices, as well as ethnic differences in levels of need achievement, and other psychosociological variables (Caudill and DeVos 1956, 1960, 1965, 1968; Child, Storm, and Veroff 1958; Rosen 1963; Guthrie 1968; Gallimore 1969; Ramírez and Price-Williams 1974; Gray 1975; Gould 1980; Kagan and Knight 1981; Gardner 1983).

The comprehensive study of need achievement (N-Ach) that over the last thirty years emanated from a general interest in human motivation matched with a desire to discover a method for empirically measuring the strength of an individual's motives to achieve. Prior to the first work on need achievement (McClelland, Atkinson, Clark, and Lowell 1953), learning theorists were concerned with the experimental study of motivation, primarily in animals. However, psychoanalytically oriented psychologists and psychiatrists (McClelland 1953, Murray 1953), who were dealing with the study of human motivation, found the bases for their conclusions in clinical rather than experimental research. There was limited development in the area of experimental study of human motivation mainly due to the fact that there were no satisfactory objective measures of significant human motives. McClelland's first goal was to develop a method of measuring individual differences in human motivation (which would be) firmly based on the methodology of experimental psychology and the psychological insights of Freud and his followers (McClelland 1961).

Another extensively used method of eliciting fantasies of the individual that reveal motivations is Henry Murray's thematic apperception test (TAT) (1953). Both of these clinical methods have been censured for a lack of rigorous quantitative methodology for determining the strength and extent as to which motives were operating in a person's life. There was the need to integrate the experimental perspective with the clinical views. Within this framework, McClelland's team of researchers made the attempt to objectively quantify human motivation reflected in TAT responses, consistent with the experimental perspective.

McClelland's Achievement Motivation Theory

McClelland initiated his research project of motivational measurement along the lines of the Hullian paradigm. Just as Hull (1943) had experimentally manipulated drive states in animals (e.g., he augmented the hunger drive by depriving animals of food for varying lengths of time), McClelland experimentally manipulated the strength of food motivation in humans. He gathered TAT stories from subjects who had experienced varying degrees of food deprivation. The experiments indicated that different degrees of hunger were reflected in different amounts of food imagery in the TAT stories. It was concluded that fantasy TAT stories could also be used to measure the strength of motivation (Atkinson and McClelland 1948).

Subsequent to this study, McClelland concentrated directly on the subject of achievement motivation, one of the motives previously defined by Henry Murray. These initial studies were conducted with middle-class males from Wesleyan University. In order to vary the intensity of achievement motivation, McClelland devised three sets of instructions, one of which was given to the subjects just before they began the TAT test. The experiment group was informed that individuals who performed successfully on the fantasy test were prominent businessmen and administrators. The instructions were assumed to enhance the production of achievement-oriented responses. The responses of this group were compared to responses of a group who were given "neutral" instructions, while a third group was given a "relaxed" set of instructions. The specific kinds of thoughts that were present in the achievement group TATs and absent in the "neutral" and "relaxed" set of TATs became the operational definition of achievement motivation (McClelland 1953). One of the most frequently cited conclusions of this research is that the data we have to date strongly support the hypothesis that achievement motives develop in cultures and families where there is an emphasis on the independent development of the individual. However, low achievement motivation is related to families in which the child is more dependent on his parents and subordinate in importance to them. Due to the important nature of this statement and its effect on subsequent research, it will be discussed here in some detail.

Motives are different patterns of thought associated with different goals. McClelland (1955) defined achievement thoughts as those associated with striving for some degree of excellence in an endeavor, as contrasted with thoughts associated with the acquisition of prestige and influence (power motivation), or thoughts associated with friendly relationships (affiliation motivation). According to McClelland, a TAT story reflects the achievement motive if, and only if, it includes a stated goal of striving for a standard of excellence. Achievement goal imagery (AI) is reflected in any one of the four types of AI: competition with others, competition with one's self, striving for some unique accomplishment, and long-term involvement. Following McClelland's initial seminal work, studies have been conducted to explore further the nature, relevance, and effects of achievement motivation. Researchers in this area maintain that individuals with high achievement motivation tend to respond in certain characteristic ways:

> 1. Persons with high need achievement express preference for situations in which they can secure

concrete, immediate feedback in order to evaluate their performance (French 1958, Moss and Kaga 1961).

2. They express a preference for situations in which they can take personal responsibility for the outcome of their efforts. They seek control of their own destinies through their own actions, innovations, and initiatives (McClelland 1953, French 1958).

3. Such individuals express a preference for maintaining carefully calculated moderate-risk goals. They do not set extremely high-risk and extremely low-risk goals in which their failure appears inevitable or are guaranteed of success. They chose challenging goals where the outcome is most uncertain (McClelland 1953, Atkinson and Litwin 1960).

The pattern which emerges from these action strategies is frequently characteristic of people in entrepreneurial positions where calculated risks are encouraged, and self-reliance and initiative are valued (McClelland 1961).

Cultural Context of Achievement

Subsequent to the extensive work on need achievement, the research literature on N-Ach among different cultural groups shows a tendency that parallels high N-Ach with competitiveness and low N-Ach with cooperativeness. A different pattern shown in this study suggests a trend in achievement potential modes indicating that higher-achieving Puerto Rican students tend to have greater achievement potential modes irrespective of whether via conformance (cooperativeness) or via independence (competitiveness).

Supporting this relationship, Kagan and Knight (1981) comparing social motives between Anglo and Mexican American students, found that the cultural differences in cooperation-competition are related to those in N-Aff and N-Ach. Gould (1980) also found a significant correlation between N-Ach and upward mobility in Mexican American college students.

During the initial period of McClelland's work in achievement motive with American subjects, CaudilI (1952), Caudill and DeVos (1956), and DeVos (1960, 1965, 1968) focused on the dynamics of the achievement motive in relation to individuals of Japanese and Japanese American background. One of the reasons for the interest in the American-born Nisei stemmed from their occupational and social adjustment despite the pervasive atmosphere of ethnic and racial discrimination during World War II. In the samples of TAT data obtained by DeVos in Japan, there appeared to be a decisive preoccupation with achievement and accomplishment irrespective of where or what group of Japanese was tested (in terms of level of acculturation). Contrary to the McClelland-Atkinson model, the achievement imagery differed from that of the American samples: throughout the Japanese TAT reports there was the expression of high need for affiliation concomitant with a high need for achievement. In the work with American subjects, it was generally reported that there was an inverse relationship between the appearance of need achievement and need affiliation.

It is McClelland's contention that a nation's economic progress is perpetuated by the persistence of high need achievement and the existence of entrepreneurial values of self-reliance and independence throughout the population. Need achievement is ideally embodied in a socially mobile, expediential, instrumentally oriented personality type dedicated to the pursuit of selfish gain (DeVos 1968).

DeVos (1968) assumes that McClelland's model may well suit American culture, but that it is less applicable for those culture that train children to seek familial and social rewards via need affiliation rather than need achievement. He points to the Japanese economic and social development that depends not only on individual endeavors and perseverance for personal aggrandizement, but he also contends that it was the concerted cooperative efforts that led to the rapid change in Japanese economic development. DeVos emphasizes the need for viewing the total cultural configuration and the various alternative roles through which achievement motivation is directed.

The notion is that achievement may be motivated by such factors, as need affiliation is important. More attention must be paid to situational variables than has been typical of achievement studies. It is probable that situational cues will be more important determinants of achievement.

Success for oneself only was considered a sign of excessive immoral egoism in Japan (DeVos 1968). Instead, the individual is expected to achieve for the benefit of the family. DeVos (1960) reports that the subjective sense of need to repay the parents for their self-sacrificing care is an impetus for the individual in the Japanese family to maintain a high standard of achievement. The nature of group cohesiveness, the strong sense of dedication of individual Japanese and group processes within the Japanese community make it imperative to reexamine the strong need for social belonging and affiliation as it affects need achievement in different cultural groups.

Child, Storm, and Veroff (1958) applied McClelland's methodology to the study of child-rearing patterns as a reflection of cultural values. To establish this relationship, Child examined ethnographic data on child-rearing practices from a total of fifty-two cultures. Folktales, which are told to children during the socialization process within these cultures, were analyzed and used as the measure of cultural values. The cultures that they characterized as "rigid" or "restrictive" in child-rearing practices (punishing children for failure to be obedient and responsible) were said to have folktales with relatively low levels of achievement motivation. Those cultures that were characterized as "more lenient" and "less punitive" were said to have folktales with relatively numerous of high-achievement themes.

Rosen (1962) also used McClelland's TAT scoring system to explore differences in samples of Brazilian and Americans. He concluded that variations in socialization practices are the principal factors that are attributable to differences in achievement behavior in both cultures. A comparison of the two cultures led Rosen to believe that American culture stresses independence, self-reliance, autonomy, and induces the child to compare himself competitively with idealized standards of excellence.

Parker (1962) followed a similar methodological design in the analysis of Eskimo and Ojibwa mythology in terms of need achievement. From his analysis, the Ojibwa culture reflects a greater amount of stress on individual achievement as compared with the Eskimos, whose culture reflects a concern with affiliation rather than individual striving for achievement.

The aforementioned findings are in agreement with the study by Atkinson and O'Connor (1966), which illustrated that high-need affiliation, low-achievement-oriented individuals were induced to behave in an achievement-oriented fashion when social approval was available. They concluded as follows:

This hypothesis means that a person in whom the achievement motive is very weak (a person who produces very little imagery having to do with excellence of performance in thematic apperceptive stories under neutral conditions) might display all the behavioral symptoms of an entrepreneurial risk-taker if some extrinsic reward like love or money, for which he does have a strong motive, were offered as a general inducement for performance (Atkinson and Feather 1966).

It seems that for some individuals, the important issue for them is social approval and not competition with a standard of excellence; these persons would be more concerned with what others thought of their behavior rather than what they thought themselves.

Gallimore (1969) examined the following hypothesis: "For members of a cultural group for which social approval is a salient environmental cue, increases in the amount of achievement-oriented behavior (preference for intermediate risks) can be obtained by manipulating the availability of social evaluation and, by implication, social approval" (Kubany 1969). Gallimore focuses his attention on ethnic groups in Hawaii since Hawaiians have been characteristically regarded as "low achievers" in all spheres of life. Thus, the hypothesis that poor achievement in the schools, for example, could be accounted for in the Hawaiian case by low levels of achievement motivation is often expressed by teachers and administrators. The TAT was administered to high school males, and the responses were scored following usual procedure as outlined by Atkinson (1958). As was expected, the Hawaiian groups scored lower on fantasy need achievement than any of the other comparison groups of Japanese Americans, Afro Americans, and Filipinos. Of particular interest is the lack of need-achievement theme within the urban Hawaiian samples; this group came from a private school specifically established to serve children of Hawaiian descent who displayed high academic potential. It appeared the TAT pictures elicited little need-achievement imagery from Hawaiian students, irrespective of their success in school. These findings led Gallimore to address the question of what motives are important to Hawaiians other than need achievement, which might potentially be used to account for variations in achievement within the Hawaiian group. The answer to this question was found in the works of Gallimore and Howard (1968) and Gallimore, Howard, and Jordan (1969) that indicated that affiliative concerns are extremely important in any description of Hawaiian socialization practices and behavioral development.

The work of Gallimore (1969) deserves a greater attention. In an attempt to test his proposition, he selected a population of Filipinos living in Hawaii. The genesis of this work was a pilot study concerned with the values, behaviorial patterns, and child-rearing practices of Filipinos. Those observers who were involved in the pilot project noted the importance attached to their informants to social approval, interpersonal harmony, and to meeting the perceived expectation and needs of others. Other support for this study is found in the work of Whiting (1963), Lynch (1964), Guthrie and Jacobs (1966), and Guthrie (1966). Whiting, for example, stated that Filipinos are socialized to be responsive to the expectations of others and, in particular, to members of their nuclear and extended family. From these studies one may conclude that Filipinos tend to be less affected by "internalized motives" for achievement motivation. It appears that Filipinos do not tend to strive so much for the self-satisfaction that it may generate but rather, because such success will please others, bring honor to the family and secure one's safety from the shame of public failure. In short, according to Gallimore (1969) it may be that achievement and achievement-oriented behavior among Filipinos are more affected by "situational cues" than by intrinsic ones (a motivational disposition such as need achievement).

Ramírez and Price-Williams (1974) found results similar to Atkinson's, which further illustrates the limitations of the McClelland construct of achievement motivation. In their study, Mexican American and Anglo-American children were asked to respond to the school-situation picture stories. Their responses were analyzed for need achievement. Anglo-American children scored higher on need achievement (as defined by McClelland, Atkinson, Clark, and Lowell 1953), and Mexican American children scored higher on need achievement for the family. That is, stories told by traditional Mexican American children indicated that they wanted to achieve so that their families might benefit from their achievements. In contrast, stories told by Anglo-American children reflect need achievement for self, in which the achiever is the primary beneficiary.

A retrospective view of the work of DeVos (1968), Horner (1968), Gallimore (1969), Ramírez and Castañeda (1974), and Gray (1975) set the challenge for psychologists and other social scientists interested in cross-cultural studies of achievement and achievement motivation in conceptual as well as methodological terms. As DeVos (1968) states, the study of achievement motivation must be seen as part of the total cultural context that may spur or inhibit achievement. Cross-cultural comparison of need achievement, whether a total societies or minority segments of particular societies, is meaningless without due attention to the complex differences of both cultural personality configurations involved. There is obvious need for the development of techniques as represented by the work of McClelland and his associates for quantitative measurement of the relative degree concerned with achievement motivation. We must also, however, apply quantitative measures to other aspects of the cultural context to adequately gauge interrelationships of need achievement, economic and intellectual development .

In his work on intellectual development, Gardner (1983) suggests that there is persuasive evidence for the existence of several human intelligences, and these are relatively independent of one another, and that they can be fashioned and combined in a multiplicity of adaptive ways by individuals and cultures. In this work, Gardner challenges the prevailing notion of a single intelligence and puts forth a different view of human intellectual competences. Gardner argues that we are all born with the potential to develop a multiplicity of intelligences, most of which have been overlooked in our testing society, and all of which can be drawn upon to make us competent individuals. The potential for musical accomplishment, bodily mastery, spatial reasoning, and the capacities to understand ourselves as well as others are, Gardner argues, the multiple forms of intelligence that we must add to the conventional and typically tested logical and linguistic skills long called IQ. Through his inquiry into cultural variations in cognitive competence, Gardner hopes that it will inspire social scientists to develop a model of how intellectual competences may be fostered in various cultural settings. Somewhere between the Chomskian stress on individuals, with their separate unfolding mental faculties, the Piagetian view of the developing organism passing through a uniform sequence of stages, and the anthropological attention to the formative effects of the cultural environment, Gardner suggests that a middle ground position that takes seriously the nature of innate intellectual proclivities, the heterogeneous processes of child development, and the ways in which these are shaped and transformed by the particular practices and values of culture may be forged.

As Gray indicated (1975), "one may conclude from the majority of studies presented that the dynamics of achievement motivation for those who do not belong to the group of white, male, middle-class students are not clearly delineated by the traditional McClelland-Atkinson model. In spite of the extensive influence of the above concept of achievement motivation there is a critical need for a viable theory to explain cultural differences in the drive for achievement motivation."

Inspired by the works of these researchers, specifically Gray (1975) on preferred mode of achievement motivation and Kluckhohn (1961) on value orientations, I proposed to investigate the relationship of one of Kluckhohn's five value dimensions entitled Relational Value Orientations with the Mode of Achievement Potential of Mainland and Island Puerto Rican College Students.

The impact of the two cultural systems (from the society of origin and the host society) on the relational value of orientations and the achievement potential of Puerto Rican mainlanders and islanders is a phenomenon that merited empirical attention and was therefore the focus of this study.

Whereas value orientations of numerous immigrant groups have been studied (Chan Yin [Chinese] 1978, Lopata [Poles] 1976), Feather and Wasyluk [Latvians, Ukrainians] 1973, Simoes [Portuguese] 1971, Femminella [Italians] 1968) for the general population, and Vázquez and Wurzel (1979) and Sjostrom (1983) for Puerto Ricans, the relational value orientations and the achievement potential mode of Puerto Ricans have yet to be studied.

In the area of achievement potential and motivation, current assessment measures have given little attention to the distinction between the motive to achieve and the manner in which this motive is actualized—dependent on culturally approved means and ends. However, the achievement-motivation literature emphasizes that achievement depends on a generalized desire to achieve; it does not deal with the issue of whether or not a culture values the appropriate achievement behavior. For example, initial studies of achievement motivation conducted with middle-class white males showed that high-need achievers valued achievement for self (McClelland, Atkinson, Clark, and Lowell 1953). In contrast, studies conducted in this area with Japanese Americans showed that high-need achievers were more inclined to pursue goals benefiting others, particularly the family. Success for oneself was seen as a sign of excessive immoral egoism (DeVos 1968). According to Maehr (1974), the desire to achieve is often confounded with the goal to achieve. This results in the possibility that one might exhibit behaviors characteristic of highly motivated persons, only directed to different goals that are acceptable in one culture, but not in another.

CHAPTER III

VALUE ORIENTATIONS

Florence Kluckhohn (1961), utilizing this concept of systematic variation in value orientation, states that our most basic assumption is that there is a systematic variation in the realm of cultural phenomena, which is both as definite and as essential as the demonstrated physical and biological phenomena. One way to approach the problems of cultural variation is to deal with the variability in the highly generalized elements of culture, which in this study are called value orientations.

These value preference or orientations are considered to be cultural products, and though there is considerable individual interpretation and meaning within a given group, the values are not randomly preferred but systematically selected. Although individuals within a given society do not always share the same rank ordering of values, there is a consistent pattern within a particular society that represents the dominant value-orientation profile of that society (Parsons 1951, C. Kluckhohn 1953, DuBois 1955, Williams 1960, Falling 1965, and Rokeach 1968). Subsequent literature lends support to the theory of systematic variation in value orientation and the fact that any change that occurs in value systems takes considerable time and the consensus of the particular sociocultural group. It is not, therefore, random or individually incorporated into the value structure (F. Kluckhohn 1951). F. Kluckhohn (1953) further elaborates that the distinctive quality of each culture and the selective trends that characterize it rest fundamentally upon its system of value orientations, and that is primarily by the transmission of their values that cultures perpetuate themselves.

Adding to these points, DuBois (1955) states that the viability of a value system does not rest exclusively on its internal coherence. It must also manifest a considerable degree of congruence with the situational context within which it exists. Changes in value systems will result, therefore, from a strain for consistency not only within the value system, but also between values and situational factors.

Beyond the placement of value orientations for a given society within the context of the sociohistorical influences affecting the selection of a particular rank ordering of values for that society, the area of the stability of values over time must be analyzed. Most literature dealing with change or variation in value orientations attests to the basic stability of the system with certain changes in behavior or attitudes on the part of individuals or groups within a society. The work of Rokeach and Feather are of particular importance in defining the areas of attitude, belief, and values, and the differences between these concepts. They, along with Williams (1960), have promoted thorough studies of values as the core concepts in understanding human behavior. Williams (1960) states that it is a rare and limiting case if and when a person's behavior is guided over a considerable period of time by one and only one value. More often, particular acts or sequences of acts are steered by multiple and changing clusters of values. After a value is learned, it becomes integrated somehow into an organized system of values wherein each value is ordered in priority, with respect to other values. Rokeach (1973) further elaborates that such a relative conception of values enables us to define change as a reordering of priorities and, at the same time, to see the total value system as relatively stable over time.

In the seminal work of F. Kluckhohn, it is pointed out that all societies or cultures have a dominant value-orientation profile, which represents the values held by a majority or the most powerful elite within that society. There are also variant profiles within all societies that represent the views of individuals or groups whose choices for desirable behavior vary from those of the ruling or dominant group. An example of the type of variation in value orientations from the dominant profile within the context of the United States society are found in certain ethnic or religious groups such as Mexican Americans and Mennonites. Williams (1968) has established criteria for determining the dominant values for a group or social system as follows:

> 1. *Extensiveness of value in the total activity of the system.* What proportion of a population and of its activities manifest the value?
>
> 2. *Duration of the value.* Has it been persistently important over a considerable period of time?
>
> 3. *Intensity with which value is sought or maintained.* As shown by effort, crucial affirmation, and by reactions to threats to the value.
>
> 4. *Prestige of value carrier.* That is, of persons, objects, or organizations considered to be bearers of the value.

Dominant and variant value orientation profiles are of importance to this study since the two target groups, mainland and island Puerto Ricans, constitute an ethnic group in American society, and their native cultural ethos differs considerably from that of the host society, the United States.

VARIATIONS IN VALUE ORIENTATIONS

The subject of variations in value orientations was researched initially by F. Kluckhohn (1961), who postulated a theory based on the works of Parsons and C. Kluckhohn.

The major premise of Kluckhohn's theory of values orientation is that there is universality in some human problems and an ordered variation in value-orientation systems within all societies. C. Kluckhohn (1951) provided the basis for the development of this theory from Parson's theory of action, contending that there is a philosophy behind the way of life of each individual and of every relatively homogeneous group at any given point in their histories. This gives, with varying degrees of explicitness, some sense of coherence or unity both in cognitive and affective dimensions. The underlying principles arise out of, or are limited by, the givens of biological human nature and of the universalities of social interaction. All too frequently, those who have ably demonstrated a uniqueness in the values systems of different societies have ignored the fundamental fact of the universality of some human problems and its correlate that human societies have found from some problems approximately the same answers.

F. Kluckhohn (1961) postulated that all or almost all aspects of the social life of a people give expression in varying ways and varying degrees to be sure to the basic values that are characteristic of one culture as opposed to another. She then, in collaboration with F. Strodbeck, developed an instrument for systematically measuring the similarities and differences in value-orientation preferences within a particular group and between two or more cultural groups. The instrument, known as the Kluckhohn value-orientation schedule (KVOS) was field-tested with several ethnic groups in the Southwest, which included a Texas homestead community, a Mormon village, a Navajo tribe of the Zuni pueblo, and a group of Spanish Americans from the village of Atrisco, New Mexico, in order to ascertain the existence of patterns of variations among people of different cultures and subcultures. The findings supported the contention of within-group consensus and between-group differences among the groups investigated.

The KVOS deals with four basic value areas that are central to all human groups. They are summarized by the following questions:

1. What is the relation of the individual to nature? (People-Nature orientation)

2. What is the temporal focus on human life? (Time orientation)

3. What is the modality of human activity? (Activity orientation)

4. What is the modality of the individual`s relationship to others? (Relational orientation)

The classification of possible value orientation alternatives within these areas is based on the following assumptions:

1. There is a limited number of common human problems for which all people at all times must find some solution.

2. While there is variability in solutions of all the problems, it is neither limitless nor random but is definitely variable within a range of possible solutions.

3. All alternatives of all solutions are present in all societies at all times but are differentially preferred (Kluckhohn 1961).

Rokeach (1973) concurs that the conception of human values is guided by similar assumptions:

1. The total number of values that a person possesses is relatively small.

2. All people everywhere possess the same values to different degrees.

3. Values are organized into value systems.

4. The antecedents of human values can be traced to culture, society, and its institutions and personality.

5. The consequence of human values will be manifested in virtually all phenomena that social scientists might consider worth investigating and understanding.

Table 1 illustrates the four value orientations utilized in Kluckhohn value-orientation schedule and the range of variations postulated for each. This schedule in its present form measures orientations in these four areas, although an additional area of human-nature orientation formed part of the original research project.

Since for the purpose of this study, only the relational orientation is being considered, specific attention is given to this particular value orientation in this section.

TABLE 1
THE FOUR VALUE-ORIENTATIONS AND THE RANGE OF
VARIATIONS POSTULATED FOR EACH

ORIENTATION	POSTULATED RANGE OF VARIATIONS		
Man-Nature	Subjugation to Nature	Harmony with Nature	Mastery over Nature
Time	Past	Present	Future
Activity	Being	Being in Becoming	Doing
Relational	Lineality	Collateralism	Individualism

RELATIONAL VALUE ORIENTATION

This orientation defines the individual's relationships to others and provides three alternatives: lineal, collateral, and individualistic. When the lineal alternative is dominant, there is a primacy as an ordered positional succession (Kluckhohn 1961). Lineality prevails in societies where roles are ascribed and representative. A collateral orientation calls for a primacy of the goals and welfare of the laterally extended group. The individual is not a human being except insofar as he or she is part of a social group. When the Individualistic principle is dominant, individual goals have primacy over the goals of the group, and each individual's responsibility to the total society and his or her place in it are defined in terms of goals and/or roles that are autonomous. The work of F. Kluckhohn has been utilized in this study as a means of looking at the relationship between relational value orientations and mode of achievement potential of mainland and island Puerto Rican college students.

Sjostrom (1983), for instance, in her comparative study on Americans and islander and mainlander Puerto Ricans value orientations, found significant similarities between islander and mainlander Puerto Ricans in the collateral toward individualistic relational value orientations.

In a study of informational systems and value orientations of Portuguese, Portuguese American, and American students, Simoes (1971) found that culture and chronological age seem to be variables that determine value orientations in the "Kluckhohn inventory." He further concluded that the relational value-orientations data directs the Portuguese sample in the area of lineality. The type of responses seemed to be related to the order in which the leader kept the society and/or family together. In contrast, the American and the Portuguese American groups emphasized the theme of working together or being your own boss and of doing what one wants to do. Simoes (1971) concluded that judging from the information received from the Kluckhohn inventory, the children with different cultural backgrounds do have a different approach to society.

Wurzel (1979) found statistical significant difference on mean scores of the lineality and individuality subdivisions on relational value orientations between Puerto Ricans and Anglo Americans. He also found that sex differences do not appear to be a strong factor in value orientation responses for these samples.

VALUE-ORIENTATION PROFILE

This subsection reviews the literature on cultural ethos components of contemporary United States and Puerto Rican societies. The value-orientation profile of second-generation mainland Puerto Ricans is analyzed from the perspective of cultures in contact and the impact of acculturation of this particular group.

The literature on value orientation patterns or profiles encompasses the macroperspective of national or societal value systems and the microperspective of individual value profiles or subsystems. These subsystems may be representative of the dominant or prevailing value orientations of the society at large or may be variant from the dominant profile. Parsons (1951) states that every social system, even a total society, has a paramount value pattern. This, in turn, is differentiated by a process he calls "specification" to constitute values for the various differentiated and segmented subsystems of the larger system.

The importance of comprehending the value-orientation profiles across cultures facilitates access to the world view (Weltanschaulng) of different cultures and offers explanatory power to the behavioral patterns manifested as a result of the underlying value system. As F. Kluckhohn (1961) explains, all or almost all aspects of the social life of people give expression in varying degrees to be sure to the basic values that are characteristic of one culture as opposed to another. As far as continuity through time, it is a fact known to anyone who has become seriously engaged in cross-cultural studies that the ideas and techniques a people either borrow from or have been forced upon them by another culture are far more often adapted to the old ways of thinking and acting than they are disruptive of those ways.

AMERICAN VALUE-ORIENTATION PROFILE

Several historians believe that early in American historical development, Anglo-Saxon values and cultural norms were institutionalized as "American norms" and as "acceptable" standards of behavior. They were perpetuated and transmitted through the socialization and enculturation of subsequent generations of their descendants (Handlin 1953, Kluckhohn 1961, Dinnerstein 1975). One shortcoming of analyzing the value orientations of American society solely from the perspective of Anglo-Saxon Protestant values is that it omits the dynamic interactive process of value formation and change as influenced by many cultures that have come into contact in the United States. It is believed that the Anglo-Saxon influence historically has had a more profound impact on the universal culture than any other single ethnic group. However, this influence can be overstated in terms of the general American culture. European cultures were themselves influenced by African and Asian cultures before the European explorers started coming to the Americas in the fifteenth century. Furthermore, the Native American influence on the original English immigrants to the New World was extensive and can be seen in many present-day customs. To the extent that there is a general or universal culture in the United States, it has resulted from a series of multiple acculturations based on the constant culture contact created by the massive immigration to the United States since its emergence as a nation.

Although extensive literature on the value orientations of American society supports a uniform Anglo-based profile with roots in the British immigration during colonial times (DuBois 1955, Weber 1558, F. Kluckhohn 1961, Williams 1968), the influence of a wide variety of immigrant cultures must also be considered as an influence on the cultural ethos of modern United States society (Bernard 1956, Femminella 1969, Glazer and Moynihan 1975). The former position clearly supports the constancy of certain values patterns over time, even though cultures are in contact with each other and subject to change. The latter suggests that ethnic ideological themes are constant, given the multiple acculturations and the influence of impact-integration or emergent culture theories (Sjostrom 1983).

Miller (1972) has delineated several trait clusters that are believed to constitute a profile for a given national culture. Among these are the areas of concern for and trust of others, family solidarity, definition of religion and moral conduct, consensus over general philosophy and objectives of the society, definition of work, and individual achievement. These clusters subsume the Kluckhohn categories of time, relational, man-nature, and activity orientations respectively.

The value orientations of a given culture reflect that group's assumptions concerning their view of the universe, people's relation to the universe, individual development, and relations to others in society. Therefore, an examination of the relational value orientations will generate the parameters of expected similarities and differences of mainland and island Puerto Rican groups and will provide a point of departure for interpreting the influence of these two cultural entities on the value system of second-generation Puerto Ricans born and reared in the United States.

Value configurations are ideal types, which represent tendencies and do not encompass within-group differences typical of any given society. However, they serve to point out particular regularities or patterns of value orientation and will be utilized as a means of looking at the dominant value-orientation patterns of the aforementioned groups.

The United States, whose societal value orientations can be traced to the White Anglo-Saxon Protestants who inhabited this country during the colonial period, has been credited with instituting four main value orientation patterns. These are described by Williams (1960) as the democratic ethos, with its stress on prosperity, freedom, and individualism; the belief in private economic enterprise, with the associated traits of activity and work, achievement and success, and material comfort; Judeo-Christian beliefs, with Protestantism dominating; and secularism, with an emphasis on progress, and scientific and technological achievement. He further describes American culture as one, which deemphasizes the past and orients strongly to the future. While at first glance these may appear as configurations for many societies, several stand out as appearing throughout the literature specifically addressing American value orientations. They are as follows: achievement, activity, efficiency, individualism, competition, progress, and control over nature. These values all fit within the categories of relational, time, activity, and people-nature orientations established by F. Kluckhohn.

DuBois (1955) has stated that the value premises of any culture can be considered to rest upon the assumptions made concerning people's cognitive view of the universe, people's relation to it, and people's relation to others. For the American middle class, it is postulated that the universe is mechanistically conceived and the individual is its master. In the context of the past three hundred years of American history, these assumptions have proved valid both experientially and integratively for the United States as a whole and specifically for the large American middle class.

There is a basic consensus across the literature that a particular pattern of Anglo values emerged resulting from the sociohistorical and economic growth of the United States as a modern, industrialized nation with a predominantly capitalistic economic system and a philosophical tradition of pragmatism.

The salient value-orientation pattern for American society consists of a number of orientation categories. The first, relational, emphasizes the individual and his or her responsibility in taking the initiative to succeed and consider his or her own interests and needs above those of the collectivity. Within this category, the individual is expected to be independent, industrious, thrifty, and motivated to achieve. The second deals with the view of human beings' role within the universe, and the American or Anglo model is one of active mastery in controlling the forces of nature through scientific discovery. In the time sphere, the Anglo pattern tends to be future oriented, with a strong focus on planning ahead. The activity dimensions demonstrates a concentration on the external material aspects of things and events rather than on the inner experience of meaning and effect, which would be typical of Eastern cultures. Social order and organization are an inherent part of the activity dimension and are considered essential to the maintenance of a technological society (DuBois 1955, Mason 1955, Williams 1960, F. Kluckhohn 1961, Fitzpatrick 1971).

The basic value-orientation patterns of American culture as we know it today are based on the principles of action and mastery over the physical world, as seen in the territorial expansion of the United States, and a concern for social mobility and progress, as evidenced by an ever-increasing technology. A view toward the future is seen in the space program and other scientific advances, and an emphasis on the individual is seen in the fostering of a competitive system of education and ways in which children are socialized in this society.

HISPANIC VALUE-ORIENTATION PROFILE

The typical Hispanic values have been delineated as being oriented toward the past or present rather than the future, emphasizing the extended family and the individual within the context of the collectivity (relational orientation), resignation or acceptance of destiny, and a focus on being or internal aspects of life rather than on doing or external aspects (Gillin 1955, Wagley 1968, Leavitt 1974).

Modern Latin-American society, which is comprised of many diversified countries, heterogeneous in their intergroup cultural characteristics, has certain common unifying themes that represent a legacy from Spanish colonialism in the New World. The works of Gillin, Williams, Fillol, and Wagley attest to certain differential patterns that make the Latin-American cultures distinct from their counterparts in the United States. Gillin (1955) states that the Latin-American cultures seem to have a common general framework and a common tone that enables them to be seen collectively as a cultural design distinctive from that of other varieties of Western civilization.

According to the literature, the major ethos components of the various Latin-American countries consist of respect for the individual, a concept of people in a society that is hierarchically organized, and a transcendental or idealized view of the world and how people should deal with reality.

Gillin (1955) provided a comprehensive picture of the major cultural ethos components of modern Latin-American culture by emphasizing those factors that he believed gave an underlying unity to modern Latin-American culture. He sustains that Latin Americans place a high value upon individuality but contends that this notion is viewed from a perspective that is radically different from that of American culture in which each person is valuable because of a unique inner quality of worth. The democratic` credo, on the other hand, holds (at least ideally) that the individual merits respect because it has to be considered just as good as the next person. Latin Americans, like other Catholics and Protestants, believe that every individual has a soul and that the soul has intrinsic worth, and thus the individual is unique (Leavitt 1974). In spite of their particular individuality, personal relationships are very important for Latin Americans, and they are established on the basis of kinship, ceremonial kinship such as *compadrazgo*, and more friendship between individuals. According to Gillin, (1955), friendship is the essential element of interpersonal relations in the Latin-American culture.

Many sociologists have agreed that Latin Americans, on the whole, are as inclined toward pragmatic, materialistic, or utilitarian considerations as their North American counterparts, they regard work as necessary, but there is also an acceptance of one's position in society and an adaptation to the established order (Gillin 1955, Leavitt, 1974).

Puerto Rican Value-Orientation Profile

In order to discuss Puerto Rican value orientations, one must view the society within the context of the Spanish cultural heritage and the industrialization and urbanization that took place subsequent that the United States took possession of Puerto Rico in 1898. It is necessary to view the processes of industrialization against the background of cultural traditions of the island. For four centuries, the culture has been essentially Hispanic both in its national institutions and its folk aspects. The Hispanic heritage has been the basis of Puerto Rican culture and subcultures, and despite the effects of industrial trends, many features of the tradition survive: the Spanish language, certain familial and educational patterns, religious practices, forms of recreation, food, habits, and others.

The literature on Puerto Rican values supports the presence of a Hispanic ethos in Puerto Rican society as outlined previously. This consists basically of the extended family structure, a past-present orientation, an emphasis on personalism (individual within the larger context of the collectivity), people controlled by destiny and/or nature, (Brameld 1958, Fitzpatrick 1971, Cooper 1972, Steward 1972, Maldonado-Denis 1976).

According to Fitzpatrick (1971), four major influences have contributed to the structure of family life, kinship patterns, and the patterns of family living in Puerto Rico: the culture of the Taino Indians, natives of the island when Columbus arrived; the influence of the Spanish colonial culture; the existence of slavery on the Island; and the influence of the United States and of economic development and modernization. While it is difficult to assess the degree of impact of any or all these factors on modern Puerto Rican society during the post–World War II period, the industrialization of Puerto Rico has probably been the major feature in the formation of its sociocultural and political value system. In an article in *Portrait of a Society* (Méndez 1972), Steward states in support of this hypothesis that all segments of the Puerto Rican population have been influenced by industrialization, but the town and urban centers have responded most uniformly. While these new urban functions tend to create greater similarity between towns, they also differentiate the population within each town into special segments, classes, or sociocultural groups: wealthy commercial and professional personnel; civil servants, transportation workers, and services and building trade groups; and skilled and unskilled laborers. Most characteristic of these are the new middle classes of varied occupations and income. They represent a new trend, a new set of values that ascribes major importance to the symbols of personal achievement and wealth. Upward mobility in the socioeconomic hierarchy becomes a crucial goal; and individual effort, thrift, education, and utilization of governmental services and opportunities become means to the goal.

While the extent of the United States' influence on the island's society is evident, the cultural norms in Puerto Rico continue to reflect the Hispanic value orientation patterns. Maldonado-Dennis (1976) states, "Afirmamos anteriormente que Puerto Rico es una sociedad de cultura nacional vinculada histórica, étnica y linguísticamente al universo cultural latinoamericano y mas específicamente al ámbito del Caribe hispanoparlante" (As has been stated on previous occasions, Puerto Rico is a society representing a national culture placed historically, ethnically, and linguistically within the framework of a Latin-American cultural universe in general and to the Spanish-speaking Caribbean in particular [translation by Sjostrom, 1983).

The prevalence of a Hispanic value orientation profile is supported by the literature for those Puerto Ricans born and reared on the island in spite of the urbanization, industrialization, and American influence over almost a century. The profile is expected to differ from the findings of Kluckhohn's study, however, regarding the Latin-American value orientation profiles. One of the five groups used by Kluckhohn for the first testing of the value orientation theory was that of the Spanish Americans from a rural village in the Southwest United States, which she named Atrisco. The dominant orientations of this group in 1951 during preliminary use of KVOS were lineality, present time, subjugation to nature, and being. Kluckhohn predicted changes in these values as small villages such as Atrisco disappeared, and the inhabitants moved to urban centers.

Table 2 summarizes the dominant relational value orientation preferences for Americans and Island Puerto Ricans, supported by the literature.

TABLE 2

TRADITIONAL VALUE-ORIENTATION PREFERENCES
FOR MAINLAND AND ISLAND PUERTO RICANS

	Mainland	Island Puerto Rican
Relational	Individual	Collateral
Orientation	Collateral	Individual
	Lineal	Lineal

The second generation of Puerto Ricans born and reared in the United States are expected to retain aspects of value-orientation preferences of their culture of origin. This group is also expected to incorporate value orientations that more closely approximate those of the American society, the context within which second-generation Puerto Ricans are born and reared.

ACCULTURATION OF IMMIGRANT GROUPS

The effects of acculturation on immigrants and their offspring have been researched extensively within the conceptual framework of cultures in contact. Central to an understanding of the acculturation process is an analysis of what the first generation or the actual immigrants themselves and their offspring, the second generation, experience as a result of the move from one culture or society to another. One way of conducting such is to treat the two groups separately and to explore how the process affected each one differentially.

Most of the literature written about the first generation deals with the aspect of culture shock created as a result of one's being confronted with *values* and customs different from those in which one was socialized. This places the immigrants in a situation of having to make choices as how well they will adapt in the new environment. According to Greeley (1974), there are six steps in the acculturation process for immigrant groups. They are as follows: (1) cultural shock, (2) organization and emergent self-consciousness about their ethnicity, (3) assimilation of the elite in the core of dominant culture, (4) militancy toward the maintenance of an ethnic identification, (5) self-hatred and antimilitancy in an attempt to eliminate the remnants of the culture of origin, and (6) emerging adjustment or adaptation into the host society (acculturation).

The variable standing out in the acculturation of the immigrants appears to be the shared past in another culture, which gives them a point of reference passed on to their offspring in the form of an idealized view of the old country. Blu (1977) stresses the importance of this connection for the immigrants in their adaptation to the new host society stating that for members of an ethnic group, their shared past as they perceive it provides a bond between them, an image of their former behavior and experience, and often one or more guides for present activities. Feather (1979) points out that their change (immigration) is abrupt and dramatic, since in doing so they not only deal with the unfamiliar but also must face the anguish of having left behind those who had been important agents in their socialization (i.e., parents, friends from childhood). The culture they enter may be very different, thus exposing them to a new language and value system, which creates a constant need for adaptation. Handlin (1963) expressed that the newcomers were on their way toward America almost before they stepped off the boat because their own experience of displacement had already introduced them to what was essential.

Another variable that appears throughout the literature deals with the rate of acculturation as dependent upon the closeness of fit or the degree of value congruence that exists between the receiving and the immigrant cultures (Kluckhohn 1961, O'Flannery 1972, Portes 1980).

Schermerhorn (1970) states that when the ethos of the subordinates has values common to those of the superordinates, integration (coordination of objectives) will be facilitated; when the values are contrasting or contradictory, integration will be obstructed. Freedle and Hall (1975) concur in the discussion of two divergent types of subcultures that serve as models for integration of immigrant groups into the host society. These are the embedded subculture, which functions as if it were an integral part of the larger culture but with fewer rights and privileges (e.g., black Americans and Hispanic Americans), and the encapsulated subculture, which is allowed to maintain its cultural practices as long as its impact on the prevailing culture, is minimal or nonexistent (e.g., Chinese Americans and American Indians).

The vast majority of empirical studies conducted on value orientation between cultural groups has addressed the issue of congruence of values between the host and immigrant groups. Their findings support the hypothesis that there is a positive correlation between congruence of closeness of fit in value orientation profiles and the rate of acculturation for an immigrant group (Kluckhohn 1951, Caudill 1952, Fillol 1961, Simoes 1971, Kitano 1972, Dempsey 1973, Feather and Wasylux 1973, Nwabuzor 1974, Calhoun 1975, Benner 1977, Pido 1977, Yao 1978, Wurzel 1979, Sjostrom 1983). A few studies indicate that variables such as racism, discrimination, and socioeconomic status influence the rate of acculturation for immigrant groups (Segalman 1966, Rokeach 1973, Calhoun 1975, Isser 1976, Chan 1978). F. Kluckhohn (1961) states that the rate of the degree of assimilation of any ethnic group to the dominant American culture will depend in large part upon the degree to goodness of fit of the group's own rank ordering of value orientations with that of the dominant culture.

The second generation, in comparison to the actual immigrant group, has had no firsthand experience or socialization with the societal structure of the culture of origin. The culturally transmitted customs, therefore, were those selectively passed on by their parents and filtered through the immigrant's perceptions of their children's functioning within the context of the new society. F. Kluckhohn (1961) points out how this takes place with the second generation sustaining that it is the child of the immigrant family who within the family structure is socialized in accord with the dominant values of traditionalism and who—outside the family, in schools, play groups, and other associations—comes to know and feel the impact of ways of behaving, which express the dominant American values.

In order to appreciate the predicament in which the offspring find themselves in dealing with the two cultures simultaneously, Nahirny and Fishman (1965) suggest that the more intensely they rejected and despised their ethnic heritage, the more aware the children became of their ethnic identity; and by suppressing their ethnicity, they rebelled against parts of themselves. Glasser (1968) further contends that in situations where a subject has prolonged interaction with persons of different ethnic identity and identification patterns, investment in the new society encourages marginality in his ethnic identification patterns.

There is general agreement among scholars of immigration and ethnicity that the offspring of the immigrant groups generally experience greater marginality than their parents in being placed constantly in situations of choosing between the two cultures. This is a tenuous predicament since acceptance of the cultural mores of the United States often forces them to reject their own parents and family structure. Also, acceptance of the value orientation patterns of the host society has not necessarily assured them equal access to benefits of the society as illustrated by the experience of several racially mixed groups of immigrant origin (e.g., Asians and Hispanics).

Femminella (1969) and Glazer and Moynihan (1975) claim that the social systems in general and cultures in particular constantly undergo change and have an impact on each other in culture contact situations. Tirayakian (1967) states that social systems seem to come into being, develop, intermingle, and become transformed over time. Femminella (1976) further illustrates this position vis-à-vis impact-integration theory, whereby both the host and immigrant (ethnic) groups—through contact, conflict, and resolution of conflict—affect each other, thus constantly changing the "American culture."

SUMMARY

The concepts of relational value orientation and mode of achievement potential were utilized in the present study as salient features in determining the presence of the acculturation process for the second generation of mainland Puerto Ricans in comparison with the persistence of the enculturation process for island Puerto Ricans in modalities of relating to others and mode of achievement.

Within the available framework for achievement motivation, children from different ethnic groups tend to be classified as low in need achievement (Rosen 1959, Mingione 1965, Coleman 1966, Heller 1966, Carpenter 1967). The problem may be due to the fact that assessment procedures are so culture bound that they sample instances of achievement motivation associated with a given culture. It should be remembered that persistence and variation in performance are not the sole property of individuals in any given culture. In fact they are universal behavior patterns assumed to exist to the same degree across cultural groups (DeVos 1968, Maehr 1974).

Although there is extensive literature on the subjects of cross-cultural difference in value orientations as well as in achievement motivation, no study of value orientations had examined the relational value orientations to the achievement modality of mainlander and islander Puerto Ricans. This study attempted to do so by analyzing both the modality of relating to others (relational value orientations) and the mode of achievement potential (achievement for the benefit of self or achievement for the benefit of others).

CHAPTER IV

METHODOLOGY

The major research goals were as follows:

> 1. To ascertain whether a relationship exists between the variables of relational value orientations and mode of achievement potential of mainland Puerto Rican college students and their island Puerto Rican counterparts

> 2. And to examine the differences between both groups' relational value orientations and modes of achievement potential

As inferred from the aforementioned research goals, the design for this study was a cross-sectional design in which the two measurements (KVOS + CPI) were taken at one time for each sample.

THE PARTICIPANTS

Underlying the first step in the collection of data was the decision to limit the study to college students, with a focus on their first year of undergraduate studies. The rationale for utilizing the aforementioned grade level is the assumption that these students, at this level, would have already developed their basic value orientations and their mode of achievement potential.

Two sample groups, each containing a minimum of fifty participants, in the eighteen- to thirty-year age bracket, were drawn from a population of undergraduate college students at Kingsborough Community College of the City University of New York and at Colegio Universitario Tecnológico de Bayamón, University of Puerto Rico. This sample size was chosen so that power to detect a medium effect by a t-test (two-tailed) at the .05 level exceeds .80 (Cohen 1977). These institutions of higher education are considered to be comparable on the basis of the types of students who attend them and on their respective course offerings. The sample groups were designated as follows:

> 1. Mainland Puerto Ricans (individuals born and reared within the continental United States and of Puerto Rican rural and blue-collar working parentage).

> 2. Island Puerto Ricans (individuals born and reared in Puerto Rico and of Puerto Rican rural and blue-collar working parentage). Blue-collar working parentage refers to parent(s) whose labor requires physical effort directed toward the production of goods or services and whose annual income(s) do not exceed the $25,000.00 amount.

The first step in the selection of the sample was the scheduling of interviews with various administrative officers and other individuals involved in the development and administration of educational programs for Puerto Rican students in New York City as well as in Puerto Rico. The researcher met with administrative officers for the purpose of ascertaining the suitability of their institutions' participation in this study.

The sampling frame for each group was derived from a process of numbering serially the course offerings for the spring semester at the institutions and then taking a random sample of fifteen classes for the island and fifteen for the mainland. The random tables from Blalock's *Social Statistics* (1979) were applied to the list of courses. Once the thirty classes were identified, the professors who taught them were contacted in order to explain the research and request permission to recruit participants from those classes. Preliminary investigation indicated that there were about twenty students per class on the average in both U.S. and Puerto Rico universities. Therefore, by contacting approximately three hundred students in each location, the researcher obtained a voluntary sample of a minimum of fifty per setting. After permission was granted, a preliminary questionnaire (appendix A) was administered for the purpose of distinguishing the groups based on the variables of age, socioeconomic status, parentage, origin, number of years having lived outside of the United States or Puerto Rico, place of birth and rearing, and use and competency of the Spanish and English languages. Puerto Rican islanders selected were Spanish dominant, while Puerto Rican mainlanders selected were English dominant. Subjects' high school grade point averages were also considered. The completed preliminary questionnaire was reviewed, and the information obtained through this process generated the two sampling frames for the study.

It was decided that a minimum of fifty subjects from each sample would be drawn randomly from the populations contacted. Each of the one hundred and twenty-five subjects selected was contacted and invited to participate in the research. Those who agreed were sent a formal letter describing the study and what was expected of the study participants. The participants were contacted by the researcher to set up a one-hour-and-fifteen-minute meeting for the administration of the KVOS and CPI.

The size and composition of the samples, as well as the procedures for the administration of the scales, are a replication of those utilized by the authors of the instruments, Kluckhohn and Gough, as well as others who have used their instruments for empirical studies.

RESEARCH INSTRUMENTS

Two instruments were used in this study: the Kluckhohn value-orientation schedule (KVOS) and the California Psychological Inventory (CPI), which are described in this section.

THE KLUCKHOHN VALUE-ORIENTATION SCHEDULE

F. Kluckhohn (1961) developed the value-orientation schedule for testing differences, similarities, and shifts in the rank ordering of value-orientation alternatives among various cultures. This instrument was administered cross-culturally to five different groups, and the findings offered empirical evidence illustrating within-group regularities and between group differences in value orientations for the groups studied. There are rural and urban versions of the KVOS. Both versions are available in the English and Spanish languages. The islander sample was administered the Spanish form, while the mainlander sample was administered the English form. The urban form of KVOS was considered to be the most appropriate for this study based on the results of a pilot test of the instrument done by B. Sjostrom (1983) in Hormigueros, Puerto Rico. As a result, a translation was prepared by a Puerto Rican linguist. The translation was then disseminated to a panel that included a professor of Spanish language and literature, a Puerto Rican student, a bilingual educator, and one community member from the Puerto Rican community of New York City. After determining the accuracy of the translation and revising the draft in accordance with the consensus of this group, the instrument was pilot-tested with a group of fifteen Spanish speakers of Puerto Rican national origin, using the pretest, posttest method.

Each item on the urban form of KVOS delineates a hypothetical life situation that its author believes to be common in most urban societies and then poses three alternative solutions to the problem, which the respondent is asked to rank in terms of a first and second choice. There are twenty-two items in total—five items test the time value orientation, five items test the relational orientation, and six items each test the man-nature and activity orientations. Since the KVOS was designed as a means of cross-cultural testing of value orientations, the items reflect situations that are universal in type, even though somewhat variable in actual content. The results of previous cross-cultural research using the KVOS have demonstrated its usefulness and effectiveness in analyzing major cultural variations (Caudill 1952, Lahr 1968, Femminella 1969, Born 1970, Simoes 1971, Feather 1573, Calhoun 1975, Wurzel 1979, Sjostrom 1983). This is due primarily to the realm of the phenomena being tested—basic values or orientations—and the level of abstraction at which they are formulated, as well as the assumption that the instrument presents universal types of life situations, for which there are quite general and comprehensively stated alternatives or solutions. Internal consistency reliability was not assessed because of its inappropriateness for the KVOS, since there are too few items on each subscale, and reliability is, in part, a function of test length (Anastasi1981).

THE CALIFORNIA PSYCHOLOGICAL INVENTORY

H. Gough (1957) developed the California Psychological Inventory (CPI) that is intended for diagnosis and evaluation of individuals with emphasis upon interpersonal behavior and dispositions relevant to social interaction. In 1964, Gough made important revisions to this instrument, which is scaled and profiled for eighteen variables, containing 480 true-false items. Items in each scale are assigned unit weights (0–1), and raw scores are converted to standard scores with means of fifty and standard deviations of ten. The CPI can be administered either individually or in group testing. The items are printed in an eleven-page booklet, and a special answer sheet is used. The subject reads each item, decides whether he agrees or disagrees with what is said, and then marks *true* or *false* on the answer sheet. Testing time, including the reading of instructions, is ordinarily about a class hour in schools and colleges, or about forty-five minutes in individual testing. Completion of the test may occur under supervision, or a subject may be allowed to work on his/her own. The inventory has even been used on a mail-out / mail-in basis (Mac Kinnon 1962) with successful results. The CPI has been utilized with grade school children from the junior high level (Keimovitz and Ansbacher 1960, Lessinger and Martinson 1961, Pierce 1961) through high school (Davidas 1966, Snider 1966) and college (Holland 1959, Johnson and Frandson 1962, Aiken 1963, Goldschmid 1965, Domino 1967), across educational levels (Schendel 1965), and on into adult life (Canter 1963, Goodstein and Schrader 1963, Gough 1966). A clear and unequivocal goal of the CPI is to provide measures that retain their validity in cross-cultural application; as shown by the intensive efforts that have been expended in cross-cultural testing by Castro 1959; Gendre 1964 1966; Gough 1964, 1965, 1966; De Grada, Ercolani, and Terreri 1966.

Two reliability studies using the test-retest method were conducted. In one of these, two high school junior classes took the CPI in the fall of 1952 and again a year later as seniors. In the other, two hundred male adult took the test twice with a lapse of from seven to twenty-one days between testings. The test-retest correlation in achievement via conformance (Ac) was .73, while in achievement via independence (Ai) was .63.

DATA COLLECTION

The KVOS and the CPI were administered in a counterbalanced fashion. When the KVOS was administered, participants were provided with a copy of the schedule, an answer sheet, and a copy of the specific questions to be answered. Participants were invited to read the directions of the KVOS: "On the following pages you will find a set of stories or problems about things that happen in people's lives. After each of these stories are things different people do about the problems. You are asked to answer the indicated questions, selecting your first, second, and third choices in order of preference."

The procedure for administering the CPI, class III scale, consisted of handing out copies of the CPI and the answer sheet. Each participant read each of the indicated statements.

STATISTICAL ANALYSIS

The study is concerned with variations in relational value orientations and modes of achievement potential of island and mainland college Puerto Rican students. The central idea behind the hypotheses is that relational value orientations of islander and mainlander Puerto Ricans may be viewed as indicators of the modality in which their achievement potential is actualized.

Preliminary analyses were conducted assessing the effects of background factors on the dependent variables and assessing the islander and mainlander groups on the background variables. The variables of age, parental occupational status, and parental educational background were correlated with the dependent variables. Gender was cross-tabulated with the dependent variables. Differences between islander and mainlander groups were assessed using t-tests of means. It was found that the two groups differed significantly on age, high school grade average, number of college credits, and fathers' and mothers' occupations. These findings mandated that any tests between the two groups would have to be conducted using an analysis of covariance (ANCOVA), with the above-mentioned demographic variables entered as covariates for the purposes of inducing statistical controls.

HYPOTHESIS 1

Hypothesis 1 states that a positive linear relationship exists between relational value orientations and achievement potential:

> a. A positive linear relationship exists between linealistic and collateralistic value orientations and achievement via conformance (toward others).

> b. A positive linear relationship exists between individualistic value orientation and achievement via independence (toward self).

The components of hypothesis 1 were tested by the Pearson product-moment correlation coefficient using a one-tailed test (p. 05).

HYPOTHESIS 2

Hypothesis 2 states that a significant difference exists between mainland and island Puerto Rican students' mode of achievement potential:

> a. Island Puerto Ricans will show a stronger need to achieve for others (via conformance) than mainland Puerto Ricans,

> b. Mainland Puerto Ricans will show a stronger need to achieve for self (via independence) than Island Puerto Ricans.

The components of hypothesis 2 were tested by conducting a one-tailed ANCOVA (p. 05) for each dependent variable: Ac × Ai.

HYPOTHESIS 3

Hypothesis 3 states a significant difference exists between mainland and island Puerto Rican students relational value orientations:

a. Island Puerto Ricans will show stronger preferences for linealistic and collateralistic value orientations than mainland Puerto Ricans.

b. Mainland Puerto Ricans will show stronger preferences for individualistic value orientations than island Puerto Ricans.

The components of hypothesis 3 were tested by conducting a one-tailed ANCOVA (p. 05) for each independent variable: linealistic/collateralistic and individualistic relational value orientations.

Subsequent to hypothesis testing, a supplemental analysis was carried out comparing islander and mainlander samples on the activity orientation subscale of the KVOS, which measures orientations toward doing, being, and being in becoming. The ANCOVA procedures outlined above were used in the statistical analysis.

CHAPTER V

RESULTS

The results are presented in two sections: (1) an analysis of preliminary data to report relationships between subjects' demographic characteristics and the dependent variables, (2) hypothesis testing, and (3) supplementary analyses.

PRELIMINARY ANALYSIS

The preliminary analysis consisted of two tasks: first, to establish the relationship between the demographic variables and the dependent variables; second, to determine if there were any preexisting differences between the United States—and Puerto Rican-born samples in terms of demographic background. Table 3 contains the results of the correlations between the demographic and dependent variables.

TABLE 3

CORRELATIONS BETWEEN DEMOGRAPHIC VARIABLES AND MODE OF ACHIEVEMENT POTENTIAL AND RELATIONAL VALUE ORIENTATIONS

(N - 125)

Dependent Variables	Achievement Pot.		Value Orientations		
Demographics	Indep.	Conform.	Lineal	Collat.	Indiv.
Age	-.15*	-.15*	.10	-.05	.03
Income	.01	-.12	-.14	.12	.02
HS Grade Avg.	.18*	.25**	-.00	.07	-.11
No. of Credits	-.05	.16*	-.06	.06	.06
Father's Occ.	.09	.09	.26**	-.23**	-.03
Father's Educ.	.05	-.01	-.12	.15*	-.08

**p .01 *p .05

Table 3 indicates that achievement potential via independence is negatively related to age (r = -.15, p .05) and positively related to high school grade point average (r = .18, p .05). The correlations are statistically significant, but weak. There is a slight tendency for younger students who have higher high school GPAs to have higher needs to achieve via independence.

Achievement via conformance is significantly related to high school GPA (r = .25, p .01), number of college credits taken (r = .16, p .05). The relationships with number of college credits, age, and mother occupational status are weak. The relationship with high school GPA is moderate. These findings suggest that the need to achieve via conformance is related to scholastic achievement, length of time in college, and to younger students.

Lineality value orientation is positively related to fathers' occupational status (r = .26, p .01). This indicates that students from higher socioeconomic backgrounds tend to value hierarchically organized group relations. It must be kept in mind that no respondents had fathers in the lowest two categories.

Collateral value orientation is negatively related to fathers' occupational status (r = -.23, p .01) and positively related to fathers' educational status (r = .15, p .05). Since fathers' occupational and educational statuses are correlated at r = .32, the relationship between the two is modest. Occupational status negatively affects collateralism, while educational status is positively related to it.

The next step in the preliminary analysis was to examine differences between the U.S. and Puerto Rican subsamples in terms of background variables. The two samples are comparable in their income levels, and not comparable in the variables of age, GPA, college credits and parents' occupations. The island-Puerto Rican student sample was between the ages of 17-21 (see appendix A) with a mean of 1.00 and a standard deviation of 0.00. The U.S. sample contained significantly more older students.

The mean income level of the Puerto Rican sample was 1.83, with a standard deviation of 0.74. The U.S. sample had a similar mean (1.74) and standard deviation (0.80). This resulted in a t-value of 0.60, which was nonsignificant.

The occupational status of father and mother were significantly related to the students' birthplace.

Parent's occupation was ranked from 1 to 7 on Hamburgers (1958) revised occupational scale using U.S. census categories. The high-level white-collar occupational categories, such as top manager, owner of a business, or free professional were ranked 7, while unemployed, domestic service, and day laborers were ranked l. The mean occupational status of the sixty-six fathers of island-born students was 3.11, with a standard deviation of 1.08. The mean occupational status of the fifty-five mainland-born sample fathers was 2.19, with a standard deviation of 0.72, resulting in a t-value of -5.40, which was significant at the .01 level, indicating that island-born Puerto Rican students came from generally higher occupational levels than did U.S.-born students. A similar finding occurred between the samples on mothers' occupational status: of the thirty-nine island-born students who responded to the mothers' occupational status questions, the mothers had a mean occupational status of 2.39, with a standard deviation of 0.63; of the thirty-two U.S.-born students who responded to the mothers' occupational status question, the mothers had a mean occupational status of 1.81, with a mean of 0.54. The resultant t-value was -4.06, significant at the .01 level.

The Puerto Rican sample reported a mean high school GPA of 3.56, with a standard deviation of 0.53, and the U.S. sample reported a mean GPA of 2.96, with a standard deviation of 0.58, resulting in a t-value of 5.99, which was significant at the .01 level. This indicates that there are achievement differences between the two samples, differences in grading procedures between the United States and Puerto Rico, or that only the top-scoring students attend college in Puerto Rico.

The students all had thirty or fewer credits and were coded as (1) first-semester freshmen or (2) second-semester freshmen. The mean score of the Puerto Rican sample was 1.36, with a standard deviation of 0.48; the mean score of the U.S. sample was 1.67, with a standard deviation of 0.47. This resulted in a t-value of -3.58, which was significant at the .01 level.

These findings indicate that age, high school GPA, number of college credits, and occupational status would have to be statistically controlled in the comparisons between the two groups.

Hypothesis Testing

Hypothesis 1

Hypothesis 1 states that "a positive linear relationship exists between relational value orientations and achievement potentials," specifically that "a positive linear relationship exists between linealistic and collateralistic value orientations with achievement via conformance (toward others)," and "a positive linear relationship exists between individualistic value orientations and achievement via independence (toward self)." Table 4 contains the intercorrelations among the achievement orientation and relational value orientation variables.

TABLE 4

INTERCORRELATIONS AMONG THE DEPENDENT VARIABLES

(N = 125)

Dependent Variables	Conform.	Lineal.	Collat.	Individ.
Independence	.48***	-.03	.03	-.03
Conformance		.07	.00	-.06
Lineality			-.45**	-.48**
Collaterality				-.49**

**p .01

The correlations in table 4 do not support hypothesis 1. The correlation between conformance and lineality is r = .07, between conformance and collaterality is r = .00, and the correlation between individualism and independence is r = -.03, all of which are nonsignificant.

The constructs of lineality, collaterality, and individualism are all negatively related. Collaterality and lineality are correlated r = -.45, collaterality and individualism are correlated r = -.48, and lineality and individualism are correlated r = -.49. All correlations were significant at the .01 level. This indicates that a person who scores high on one relational value orientation is likely to score low on the other two dimensions, which suggests that the sample can be divided into linealists, collateralists, and individualists. This is, to some extent, an artifact of the scoring procedures, which required the respondent to rank a lineal, collateral, and individualistic answer in order from most- to least-preferred responds on each item. Nevertheless, none of these value orientations are related in any way to achievement orientations. This suggests that whether one is a linealist, collateralist, or individualist in terms of relational value orientations makes no difference in one's achievement modality.

HYPOTHESIS 2

Hypothesis 2 states that "a significant difference exists between mainland and island Puerto Rican students' mode of achievement potential," specifically that "island Puerto Ricans will show a stronger need to achieve for others (via conformance) than mainland Puerto Ricans," and that "mainland Puerto Ricans will show a stronger need to achieve for self (via independence) than island Puerto Ricans." Table 5 contains the results of the analysis of covariance of the mainland and island Puerto Ricans on achievement via conformance, with age, high school GPA, number of college credits, and family occupational status controlled. Preliminary tests indicated that the homogeneity of regression assumption underlying the analysis of covariance was satisfied.

TABLE 5

ANALYSIS OF COVARIANCE: MAINLAND- AND ISLAND-BORN PUERTO RICAN STUDENTS ON CONFORMANCE WITH AGE, HIGH SCHOOL GRADE POINT AVERAGE, NUMBER OF COLLEGE CREDITS, AND FAMILY SES COVARIATES

Group	N	Adjusted Mean
Island	64	24.41
Mainland	54	24.93

ANCOVA Summary Table					
Variable	SS	df	MS	F	Sig.
Covariates					
Age	51.57	1	51.57	2.60	n.s.
HS GPA	114.28	1	114.28	5.78	.05
Coll. Credits	76.93	1	76.93	3.89	.05
Father SES	5.65	1	5.65	0.28	n.s.
Mother SES	41.34	1	41.34	2.09	n.s.
Main Effect					
Birthplace	4.96	1	4.96	0.25	n.s.
Residual	2537.03	118	21.50		
Total	2670.41	123	21.71		

Table 5 indicates that the mean achievement by conformance adjusted score of island-born Puerto Rican students was 24.41. The mean achievement by conformance score of the mainland-born students was 24.93. The summary table of the analysis of covariance indicates that after the covariates are removed, birthplace had no significant independent effect upon achievement via conformance. The assumption of homogeneity of regression was satisfied. Table 6 contains the results of the analysis of covariance for the two samples on achievement via independence.

TABLE 6

ANALYSIS OF COVARIANCE: MAINLAND-BORN AND ISLAND-BORN PUERTO RICAN STUDENTS ON INDEPENDENCE WITH AGE, HIGH SCHOOL GRADE POINT AVERAGE, NUMBER OF COLLEGE CREDITS, AND FAMILY SES COVARIATES

Group	N	Adjusted Mean
Island	64	16.35
Mainland	54	15.17

ANCOVA Summary Table					
Variable	SS	df	MS	F	Sig.
Covariates					
Age	25.34	1	25.34	1.91	n.s.
HS GPA	26.38	1	26.38	2.00	n.s.
Coll. Credits	3.34	1	3.34	0.25	n.s.
Fathers' SES	6.54	1	6.54	0.49	n.s.
Mothers' SES	1.04	1	1.04	0.08	n.s.
Main Effect					
Birthplace	25.46	1	25.46	1.93	n.s.
Residual	1481.12	118	13.22		
Total	1664.90	123	13.53		

The data in table 6 indicates that the island-born sample had an adjusted mean of 16.35 on the achievement via independence scale. The mainland-born sample had an adjusted mean of 15.17. The summary analysis of covariance table indicates that birthplace had no significant effects upon achievement via independence, after the removal of the covariates. The data in tables 4 and 5 have demonstrated no empirical support for hypothesis 2. The assumption of homogeneity of regression was satisfied.

HYPOTHESIS 3

Hypothesis 3 states that "a significant difference exists between Mainland and Island Puerto Rican students' relational value orientations," specifically that "island Puerto Ricans will show stronger preferences for linealistic and collateralistic value orientations than Mainland Puerto Ricans," and "mainland Puerto Ricans will show stronger preferences for individualistic value orientations than island Puerto Ricans." Hypothesis 3 was tested using analysis of covariance of birthplace by value orientations using age, high school GPA, college credits, and family occupational background. Table 7 contains the results of the analysis of covariance for lineality. The assumption of homogeneity of regression was satisfied.

TABLE 7

ANALYSIS OF COVARIANCE: MAINLAND-BORN AND ISLAND-BORN PUERTO RICAN STUDENTS ON LINEALITY WITH AGE, HIGH SCHOOL GRADE POINT AVERAGE, NUMBER OF COLLEGE CREDITS, FATHERS' SES, AND MOTHERS' SES COVARIATES

Group	N	Adjusted Mean
Island	64	8.74
Mainland	54	9.59

ANCOVA Summary Table					
Variable	SS	df	MS	F	Sig.
Covariates					
Age	0.22	1	0.22	0.09	n.s.
HS GPA	0.28	1	0.28	0.27	n.s.
Coll. Credits	1.27	1	1.27	0.53	n.s.
Fathers' SES	19.04	1	19.04	7.94	.01
Mothers' SES	2.34	1	2.34	0.97	n.s.
Main Effect					
Birthplace	13.23	1	13.23	5.51	.05
Explained	36.42	6	6.07	2.53	.05
Residual	268.69	118	2.39		
Total	408.22	123	3.32		

Table 7 indicates that the island-born Puerto Rican students had an adjusted mean lineality score of 8.74, while the mainland-born students had an adjusted mean lineality score of 9.59. The analysis of covariance summary table indicates that after the covariates were removed, birthplace was significantly related to lineality, but in the opposite direction of the hypothesis. Table 8 contains the results of the analysis of covariance of birthplace on collaterality. The assumption of homogeneity of regression was satisfied.

TABLE 8

ANALYSIS OF COVARIANCE: MAINLAND-BORN AND ISLAND-BORN PUERTO RICAN STUDENTS ON COLLATERALITY WITH AGE, HIGH SCHOOL GRADE POINT AVERAGE, NUMBER OF COLLEGE CREDITS, FATHERS' SES, AND MOTHERS' SES COVARIATES

Group	N	Adjusted Mean
Island	64	11.59
Mainland	54	11.25

ANCOVA Summary Table					
Variable	SS	df	MS	F	Sig.
Covariates					
Age	0.16	1	0.16	0.07	n.s.
HS GPA	4.34	1	4.34	1.82	n.s.
Coll. Credits	2.14	1	2.14	0.90	n.s.
Fathers' SES	13.89	1	13.89	5.82	.05
Mothers' SES	1.86	1	1.86	0.78	n.s.
Main Effect					
Birthplace	2.11	1	2.11	0.89	n.s.
Residual	267.30	112	2.38		
Total	291.41	118	2.47		

Table 8 indicates that island students have an adjusted mean collaterality score of 11.59, and mainland Puerto Rican students have an adjusted mean collaterality score of 11.25. The difference was nonsignificant. Table 9 contains the analysis of covariance for individualism. The assumption of homogeneity of regression was satisfied.

TABLE 9

ANALYSIS OF COVARIANCE: MAINLAND-BORN AND ISLAND-BORN STUDENTS ON INDIVIDUALITY WITH AGE, HIGH SCHOOL GRADE POINT AVERAGE, NUMBER OF COLLEGE CREDITS, AND FAMILY SES COVARIATES

Group	N	Adjusted Mean
Island	64	9.91
Mainland	54	9.67

ANCOVA Summary Table					
Variable	SS	df	MS	F	Sig.
Covariates					
Age	0.78	1	0.78	0.24	n.s.
HS GPA	5.23	1	5.23	1.63	n.s.
Coll. Credits	0.47	1	0.47	0.15	n.s.
Fathers' SES	0.21	1	0.21	0.07	n.s.
Main Effect					
Birthplace	1.00	1	1.00	0.31	n.s.
Residual	359.67	112	3.21		
Total	367.16	118	3.11		

Table 9 indicates that the adjusted mean score for the island-born sample was 9.91 on individualism, and the adjusted mean score for the mainland-born sample was 9.67. The analysis of covariance summary table indicates that after the covariates were removed, birthplace was not significantly related to individualism.

In the testing of hypothesis 3, it was found that of the three relations specified, none was confirmed. The implications of the findings are discussed in chapter 5.

SUPPLEMENTARY ANALYSIS

For the purposes of expanding the theoretical scope of this study, analyses were made upon the being, doing, and being-in-becoming scales of the KVOS. The being scale emphasizes a present orientation to time, emphasizing spontaneity. The doing scale assesses subjects on their emphasis on using time to get things done and work toward specific goals. The being-in-becoming scale measures subjects' emphasis on using time to develop ones capabilities.

Table 10 contains the results of the analysis of covariance comparing island- and mainland-born Puerto Rican students on the being scale, controlling for demographic factors. The assumption of homogeneity of regression was satisfied.

TABLE 10

ANALYSIS OF COVARIANCE: MAINLAND- AND ISLAND-BORN PUERTO RICAN STUDENTS ON BEING WITH AGE, HIGH SCHOOL GRADE POINT AVERAGE, NUMBER OF COLLEGE CREDITS, FATHERS' SES, AND MOTHERS' SES COVARIATES

Group	N	Adjusted Mean
Island	69	8.07
Mainland	55	12.44

ANCOVA Summary Table					
Variable	SS	df	MS	F	Sig.
Covariates					
Age	51.81	1	51.81	18.44	.01
HS GPA	44.22	1	44.22	15.74	.01
Coll. Credits	30.56	1	30.56	10.88	.01
Fathers' SES	85.83	1	85.86	30.55	.01
Mothers' SES	11.34	1	11.34	4.04	.05
Main Effect					
Birthplace	349.40	1	349.40	124.37	.01
Residual	314.65	112	2.81		
Total	979.70	118	8.30		

The data in table 10 indicate the island-born students have an adjusted being score of 8.07, while the mainland-born students have a being score of 12.44. After the variance accounted for by the demographic covariates, the difference between the two groups resulted in an F ratio of 124.37, significant at the .01 level. Table 11 contains the analysis of the two groups on the doing scale. The assumption of homogeneity of regression was satisfied.

TABLE 11

ANALYSIS OF COVARIANCE: MAINLAND- AND ISLAND- BORN PUERTO RICAN STUDENTS ON DOING WITH AGE, HIGH SCHOOL GRADE POINT AVERAGE, NUMBER OF COLLEGE CREDITS, FATHERS' SES, AND MOTHERS' SES COVARIATES

Group	N	Adjusted Mean
Island	65	12.18
Mainland	54	10.31

ANCOVA Summary Table					
Variable	SS	df	MS	F	Sig.
Covariates					
Age	5.84	1	5.84	2.15	n.s.
HS GPA	9.57	1	9.57	3.51	n.s.
Coll. Credits	13.98	1	13.98	5.14	.05
Fathers' SES	2.82	1	2.82	1.04	n.s.
Mothers' SES	0.02	1	0.02	0.01	n.s.
Main Effect					
Birthplace	64.03	1	64.03	23.52	.01
Residual	304.98	112	2.72		
Total	414.02	118	3.51		

The data in table 11 indicate that the island-born students have an adjusted doing score of 12.18, while the mainland-born students have a doing score of 10.31, after the variance accounted for by the demographic covariates, the difference between the two groups resulted in an F ratio of 23.52, significant at the .01 level. Table 12 contains the analysis of the two groups on the being-in-becoming scale. The assumption of homogeneity of regression was satisfied.

TABLE 12

ANALYSIS OF COVARIANCE: MAINLAND- AND ISLAND-BORN PUERTO RICAN STUDENTS ON BEING IN BECOMING WITH AGE, HIGH SCHOOL GRADE POINT AVERAGE, NUMBER OF COLLEGE CREDITS, FATHERS' SES, AND MOTHERS' SES COVARIATES

Group	N	Adjusted Mean
Island	65	14.69
Mainland	54	13.28

ANCOVA Summary Table					
Variable	SS	df	MS	F	Sig
Covariates					
Age	10.66	1	10.66	3.94	.05
HS GPA	3.35	1	3.35	1.24	n.s.
Coll. Credits	5.80	1	5.80	2.14	n.s.
Father's SES	11.02	1	11.02	4.07	.05
Mother's SES	5.92	1	5.92	2.19	n.s.
Main Effect					
Birthplace	36.63	1	36.63	13.55	.01
Residual	302.97	112	2.71		
Total	389.70	118	3.30		

The data in table 12 indicate that the island-born students have an adjusted being-in-becoming score of 14.69, while the mainland-born students have a being-in-becoming score of 13.28. After the variance accounted for by the demographic covariates, the difference between the two groups resulted in an F ratio of 13.55, significant at the .01 level.

Thus, the supplemental analysis indicated that the island-born and mainland-born samples differed significantly on the activity value orientation, with the island-born Puerto Rican students scoring significantly higher on the doing and being-in-becoming scales, and the mainland-born students scored higher on the being scale.

Chapter VI

RECOMMENDATIONS

Summary of the Study

In an effort to study possible cultural differences in relational value orientations and achievement potential modes of island-born and mainland-born Puerto Rican freshmen college students, a sample of 125 participants, 70 island born and 55 mainland born, was administered a questionnaire containing demographic indicators, the achievement via conformance and achievement via independence scales of the California Psychological Inventory, and the relational and activity scales of the Kluckhohn value-orientation schedule.

In relation to the nature of this study and the groups sampled, it was presumed that the effects of socialization and schooling on Puerto Rican students take on vital importance. The socialization processes inherent in the United States institutions that mainland Puerto Ricans undergo foster the dominant value orientations of American society, while island Puerto Ricans undergo the socialization processes inherent in the Puerto Rico institutions, fostering dominant value orientations of Puerto Rican society. The school systems of New York City and Puerto Rico differ in curriculum goals and content, methodology, course of study, physical plants, equipment and environment (Brameld 1958, Gomez Tejera and López Cruz 1970). In view of the varying cultural ethos within each society and the different educational systems to which island and mainland Puerto Ricans are exposed to, it was expected that these two groups would differ from each other in their relational value-orientation preferences as well as in their mode of achievement potential. The problem was approached based on the assumption that mainland and island schools reinforce a modality to achieve which stresses contrasting achievement values. In order to bridge the gap between the possible dichotomy in values and achievement modality of these two different educational systems, it was necessary to undertake empirical exploration of the relational and activity value orientations and achievement potential mode differences of islander and mainlander Puerto Rican college students.

In order to develop hypotheses about value orientations and achievement potential modes among Puerto Ricans, the literature was searched regarding these variables with regard to Puerto Ricans, other ethnic groups, and within various Hispanic subgroups.

Florence Kluckhohn postulated five value dimensions, which grow out of people's efforts to solve five basic problems that are imminent in the human situation. Kluckhohn provided a schema to study configurational patterns of value orientations in a particular culture or social stratum. Value orientations are complex, patterned (rank-ordered) principles that give order and direction to human acts and thoughts as these relate to the solution of "common human" problems (Kluckhohn 1950). Several studies have been conducted that deal with differences in value orientation across cultures (Kluckhohn 1951, Simoes 1971, Wurzel 1979, Sjostrom 1983). These researchers contend that linealistic and collateralistic value orientations are related to a more rural upbringing in traditional social structure, while individualistic value orientations are more closely tied to urbanism and industrialism.

The achievement potential and motivation literature stresses that achievement depends on a generalized desire to achieve; it does not deal with the issue of whether or not a culture values the appropriate achievement behavior. Initial studies of achievement motivation conducted with middle-class white males showed that high-need achievers valued achievement for self (McClelland, Atkinson, Clark, and Lowell 1953). In contrast, studies conducted in this area with

Japanese Americans and Mexican Americans showed that high-need achievers were more inclined to pursue goals benefiting others, particularly the family (DeVos 1968, Gray 1975). More traditionally oriented students would tend to need to achieve via conformance (for the benefit of others), while more urban oriented students would tend to need to achieve via independence (for the benefit of self).

Because of these characterizations and the observation that island-born Puerto Rican college students would come from more traditional backgrounds and mainland-born students would come from more urban, industrial backgrounds, this study was conducted based on the hypotheses that island-born Puerto Rican college students would evidence more linealistic and collateralistic value orientations and an achievement potential modality via conformance, while mainland-born students would evidence a more individualistic relational value orientation and achievement potential modality via independence.

DISCUSSION OF THE FINDINGS

Among the entire sample, relational value orientations are related to socioeconomic background, with students from higher status families being more linealistic and less collateralistic than students from lower status families, although students whose fathers have more education tend to be less collateralistic than those with fathers having less education. This result is consistent with (Lahr 1968, Rosen 1959, Strodtbeck 1959) reporting significant correlations between socioeconomic status and value orientations, thus supporting the concept of systematic variation in value orientation within subgroups of a society.

The relationships between achievement potential modalities and demographic variables indicate that higher-achieving students tend to have greater achievement potential modalities, regardless of whether via conformance (toward others) or independence (toward self). Achievement modalities are moderately correlated. Although mainland Puerto Ricans were more linealistically oriented, both groups ranked collaterality as their highest preference, individuality as their next-highest preference, and lineality as their least-preferred orientation. These results show the same ranking pattern found by Sjostrom (1983). My interpretation of this is that islanders have moved away from only depending on and looking to an authority and have moved toward valuing family and community as sources for solutions to common human problems.

In addition, they probably will eventually adopt a preference for individualistic solutions while retaining as part of their bicultural identity an ability to apply collateralistic and linealistic solutions. In this present study, there were no significant differences between the two groups on individualistic value orientations.

It appears, within the dominant relational value orientation of Puerto Ricans participating in this study, that their life takes on significance in so far as they are part of the sociocultural group emphasizing the family and the individual well-being within the context of the collectivity. Since mainlander Puerto Ricans showed more significance linealistic value-orientation preferences when ethnicity and fathers' socioeconomic status were considered, they seem to be more inclined to the orientation in which the leader kept the society and/or family together, while islander Puerto Ricans emphasized more the theme of working together. With regard to individualistic value orientations in which there was no significant difference between the two groups, the sociological literature stresses that postsecondary education is the prime mechanism for upward social mobility (Parsons 1955, Clark 1966, Bourdieu and Passerson 1977). This is true in the West, the transforming East, and the third world, although increasingly less true in the West because of the inability of the labor market to absorb college graduates into the professional, technical, and managerial strata (Freeman 1976). Thus, both island and mainland Puerto Rican college students, irrespective of sociocultural setting, may be seeking upward social mobility. Apparently the effect of the mainland social structure in terms of developing individualistic value orientations in Puerto Rican students is not taking place. Unexpectedly, however, the mainland Puerto Ricans showed relational value orientation contrary to the hypothesis. Both islanders and mainlanders seem to value individuality, but with the notion that each person is valuable because of a unique inner quality of worth independent of material success. While in the United States, a major value assumption is that, in congruence with the Protestant ethic, that economic success reveals inner worth. Rather than being linealistic, island Puerto Ricans showed stronger collateralistic value orientations. Besides the effects of industrialization and urbanization, returning Puerto Rican migrants who settle mostly in the central city areas and middle-class suburbs (Hernández Alvarez 1977) constitute another source of variation within the Puerto Rican islanders dominant profile of value orientations.

In the islander sample, the students tended to come from the upper levels of the working class and from the lower middle class. The mainlander students tended to come from the lower levels of the working class, whose fathers perform semiskilled or unskilled labor but have the same income level as Islander Puerto Rican parents. The finding that mainland-born Puerto Rican students are more linealistic even with fathers' and mothers' SES controlled seems more plausible when considering the stratum of origin. It appears that the mainland Puerto Rican students who succeed in making it to college are those who are more attuned to having preference for group goals primacy over the individual goals primacy. This suggests that there is cultural transformation and alternately that the sociological phenomenon of cultural transcreativity in mainlanders and islanders value orientations is taking place, and social change in this respect is irreversible.

There are two possible explanations for the lack of differences in achievement potential modalities between island and mainland college students, neither of which is mutually exclusive. The first is that because of the tremendous movement back and forth between the mainland and the island among Puerto Ricans, there may be a cross-fertilization taking place in which mainlanders and islanders are becoming more alike. At the macrostructural level, the investment of U.S. corporations in Puerto Rico is industrializing and urbanizing the country. This would also lead to islanders and mainlanders becoming more similar in achievement potential modalities and relational value orientations. The second is that there may well be a selection process at work, especially among the island-born subsample, in that college students in Puerto Rico are likely to be the most urbanized of the island population. Contrarily, it would be expected that among college students there would be some socialization to the stratum of destination even before entry into college, thus making the samples ideologically similar even though social origins are different.

In the supplemental analysis it was found that island Puerto Rican students scored significantly higher on the doing and being-in-becoming scales, while the mainland-born students scored significantly higher on the being scale, indicating significantly different activity orientations between the mainland and island samples. The island-born sample places greater emphasis on effort, calculation, getting work done, meditation, and cognition; and the mainland sample places greater emphasis on peoplehood, creativity, resiliency, spontaneity, and immediate gratification. It seems, to paraphrase Kluckhohn (1961), that island-born Puerto Rican college students are more "Promethian" and "Appolonian," while the mainland students are more "Dionysian." Although Kluckhohn (1961) described "doing" as a highly prized American value, since then a cultural revolution has taken place (Dickstein 1977) giving increased emphasis to the "Dionysian" aspects of culture. Additionally, Lewis (1965) found that lower socioeconomic class members emphasize the spontaneous aspects of "being" relative to working and middle-class values. Thus, the activity orientation of the two samples may be both an artifact of the social-economic structure backgrounds of the two samples—even though SES was controlled in the analysis—and perhaps the fact that mainland-born youth are influenced by the Dionysian values sponsored by the heavily consumer-oriented culture present in the United States in the 1980s and 1990s.

It appears that the two samples differ significantly in value orientation in terms of linealistic/collateralistic as well as being, doing, and being in becoming, but do not differ in modes of achievement potential. It seems that an integrative or concomitant preferred mode of achievement exists for both mainlander and islander Puerto Rican college students. Also, island students seem to be more highly oriented to the achievement values encouraged by urban, industrial social structure in spite of coming from a more traditional background and by valuing being in becoming tended to be concerned with "the development of all aspects of the self as an integrated whole," while mainlander showed preference for the being value orientation, which stresses peoplehood, resiliency, and indulgence of existing desires (Kluckhohn 1961). Islanders showed more concentration in the external, material aspects of things while mainlanders showed concentration on the inner experience of meaning and effect.

IMPLICATIONS OF THE FINDINGS

The major implication of this study is of an educational nature. The data here indicate that there may be a means-ends problem in the educational program for mainland-born Puerto Rican students: "They are sufficiently motivated in their cultural modality, and yet there is no correspondence between the value orientations being utilized as the foundation for achievement development."

The mainland Puerto Rican students are exposed to a perplexed array of contrasting and conflicting values throughout their socialization, including that received through schooling. As a consequence they are recreating and transforming their value orientations. The Puerto Rican students in mainland schools confront expected behaviors upon which teachers place great priority but which conflict with the value-orientation behaviors toward which they lean in this study. The values of the mainland school system are evident in the behavior patterns imposed upon the students. They are expected, for instance, to be independent, divergent, and self-reliant. They are expected to complete by doing better than their peers, by finishing their task and exams in a specific timeframe, by speaking up assertively, and by being individualistic and future oriented. The behavioral values are, to various degrees, in contrast to behavioral values encouraged in the mainland Puerto Rican home in which these youngsters are expected, as shown in this study, to be collateralistic by being cooperative, conforming, convergent, humanistic, sharing with the well-being of the family, and collaborating with others for the well-being of the community. The conflictive contrast in value orientations and the failure to recognize, incorporate, and/or enhance the Puerto Rican students' value orientations into curricula may well be one of the reasons both Puerto Rico and the United States school systems are not working well for Puerto Rican students. Obviously, a school that does not consider students' value orientations cannot produce good results. On the contrary, the students achievement potential is being inhibited. Both islander and mainlander students are defined by and identified with their language and culture. Mainlander Puerto Rican students are being asked not only to give away their language but also to undergo a transformation in value orientations that has proven to be unproductive. This is one reason that education, in my opinion, has not worked well for them. Under the present methods of the school system, all the burden is being put on the students. Letting the student be subject to the matter, provoking unnecessary harder burden and unwilling application. This pedagogical practice has been a failing educational policy.

As far as implications for educational opportunity, there are a number of possibilities. First, it seems that social mobility is more restricted in Puerto Rico and that postsecondary education is designed for the reproduction of the middle class. For instance, in Puerto Rico the middle- and upper-class student is the one developing bilingual-bicultural proficiency. While in the United States, economically disadvantaged students are developing bilingual-bicultural proficiency. Education in the United States appears to be more open to opportunity for economically disadvantaged students albeit the failure in offering a relevant curriculum. Second, it is likely that although mainland students do not differ from island students in their achievement potential modalities, they showed more pragmatism in their activity, work orientation, and may not seek education as a rewarding investment. Whether this is a result of the value conflict or the consumerism of North American culture is not known. Yet such an orientation presents a serious challenge to mainland and island educators in designing harmonious educational programs and effective intercultural curricula.

Since both mainland and island Puerto Rican college students seem to prefer an integrative mode of achievement potential, it is necessary for both school systems to foster the development of both modes of achievement, rather than to encourage one over the other. As DeVos (1968) emphasized, the need for viewing the total cultural configuration and the various alternative roles through which each potential is developed should be taken into account. McClelland's model may well suite American culture, but it seems to be less applicable for the Puerto Rican culture, which train children to seek familial and social reward via need affiliation as well as via need achievement. If education is to be relevant to Puerto Rican students, their achievement values must be recognized and both environment and methodology shaped to correspond to their educational needs.

RECOMMENDATIONS

On the basis of the findings of this study, it is recommended that further research be conducted on achievement potential modalities and value orientations of both Puerto Rico and the United States schools. Such a study would provide a more comprehensive view on such important questions as how student populations on the island and mainland differ in terms of social origins and achievement behaviors relative to school success, whether there are differences in precursors to success in school between island and mainland populations, what factors are most important in school success, and how school personnel in the two populations could become successful in helping students go through their schooling and becoming aware of their own value orientations and the value orientations held by other individuals and groups. It is suggested that further studies be conducted in U.S. and Puerto Rico schools at different grade levels to determine the extent of the differences encouraged by both systems in terms of achievement values. It is additionally recommended that student counseling in the United States focus on student values toward themselves, their family, their studies, their work, and toward goal-oriented behavior. Counseling training programs should include a segment on cross-cultural counseling techniques so that cross-cultural understanding of motivating elements of culture be understood and utilized in counseling services. The literature on discrimination and disadvantagement is replete with discussions of issues related to means-ends educational problems encountered by multicultural learners (Lewis 1965, Passow 1966, Harvard Educational Review 1968, Hauser 1972, Kerhoff 1974). The data here indicate that there may be just such a means-ends problem in the educational program for mainland-born Puerto Rican students: "They are sufficiently motivated in their cultural modality, and yet there is no correspondence between their value orientations and the value orientations being utilized as the foundation for the educational program in which they are being placed."

In summarizing, in terms of value orientations, both mainland and island Puerto Rican college students seem to prefer value orientations reflecting ways of working in mutual collaboration rather than competition, valuing a collaborative working environment of helping each other to reach their potential, preferring a work ethic that no one be advantaged or disadvantaged by irrelevant considerations.

In addition, islander and mainlander Puerto Rican students prefer an integrative and concomitant achievement modality valuing achievement for the benefit of self as well as achievement for the benefit of the family. This result indicated that the rural/urban dimension that differentiates island-born and mainland-born Puerto Rican college students did not have an effect on their achievement potential modes.

In addition, developing training teacher programs to perceive accurately and respond appropriately to socioculture-related behavior and to provide vicarious experiential training on both the intellectual and emotional responses of teachers to cultural differences are critical and essential.

It is recommended that in the case of the education of Puerto Rican as well as other ethnolinguistic students a model that synthesizes different value orientations into one teaching-learning program be piloted. Such a model would provide a framework in which all three types of value orientations could operate. The Puerto Rican students' achievement value orientations, in other words the principles that guide their human conduct toward the pursuit of their life goals, should be included in the assessment of potential and incorporated as a part of an integrative teaching-learning model. Instruction for Puerto Ricans should be designed and structured in an ethnolinguistic, students-centered fashion and in correspondence with value orientations. For instance, schooling responsive to the linealistic value orientation requires thorough feedback immediately after the lesson or task has been implemented or the exam has been given. It is a common practice for students to come back from their classes indicating that they have taken the same exam many times and do not receive an explanation as to why they have not passed the exam in terms of errors they are repeatedly making. The instructor would only underline or note that there is an error, placing the full responsibility on the student to correct it, forcing the individualistic style on the student who may be oriented to look to an authority figure to guide his or her progress.

In addressing the problem with retention and graduation rates, there have been successful interventions. Instructional strategies that emphasize an integrative-learning model in conjunction with effective academic support and student development such as the one offer within the College Discovery Program of Bilingual Studies at Kingsborough Community College of the City University of New York are being considered for further educational development of ethnolinguistic students. Albeit that most of students were multilingual learners in need of developing college level English proficiency, the College Discovery Bilingual Studies Program at Kingsborough Community College has been yielding exceptional student learning outcomes as recognized by CUNY executive vice-chancellor Dr. Selma Botman and assistant dean Cheryl Williams (2006). Not only the College Discovery Bilingual Studies Program has been providing these exceptional academic achievement since 1976 but also provided for the social, cultural, and civic enrichment of bilingual learners, maximizing their capital knowledge and producing hundreds of bilingual/multilingual/ pluralistic graduates via the utilization of transformative pedagogies such as the ethnolinguistic approach (EA) Colón 1987), differentiated instruction (DI) Tomlinson, Kalbfleisch 1998; Vaughn 2000) along with the culturally responsive pedagogy (CRP) Ladson-Billings 1994).

The integration of school learning with lifelike experience, the release of students' natural drive and desire to learn, the fostering of exploration and adventure out of which personal uniqueness and social diversity may develop, and the valuing of life situations for choice making cannot be fully realized until educators are able to put educational goals such as the aforementioned together in some intelligible synthesis such as the integrative teaching-learning model.

The purpose of the integrative teaching-learning model is not only the preservation of traditional language and culture and acquisition of new language(s) and culture(s), but it is also the provision of the type of education necessary to enhance the ability to function in different cultural worlds.

The cultural worlds of both Puerto Rican islanders and mainlanders have undergone and are undergoing constant creation, transcreation, transformation, and change; and from an educational perspective it is important for the individuals to be able to function in whichever cultural world they find themselves and at the same time to contribute to its continued development and enrichment. Let us join proactively to advocate for a pedagogy for universal value orientations and achievement modalities where corporative and individual increased profit will not be the only main reason for our standard of living. Perhaps, it would be best to accept an integrative, interactive balance among self-worth, self-efficacy, and net worth, proceeding with parallel and complementary contributions and harvesting great collective benefits for the global community. Let us plan and implement educational models promoting legitimate and genuine schooling enabling students to overcome detrimental cultural dichotomies. Let us formulate, plan, and implement a pedagogy of self to enable students overcome cultural and societal dysregulation in order to accomplish true authenticity. A pedagogy of self that will generate self-learning and collaborative-learning experiences in ways that provide a form of liking the world through knowing it and of liking themselves and others through the learners' narratives curriculum. A pedagogy of self that will entice learners in overcoming distracting stimuli, both internal and external and realizing that there is a difference between the way the world is made and the way it is managed.

Through a pedagogy of self, educational success will be ensured by keeping students' process of growth constant, and their experiences integrated into gregarious, pluralistic, universal achievement values.

APPENDIX A

QUESTIONNAIRE

(English Version)

Instructions: Please fill out the following questionnaire carefully. It is important that you supply the information requested. Indicate a check (√) where applicable.

1. Name:_____

Age: 17–21_____ 22–26_____ 27–30_____ 31 or older_____

2. Sex: female_____ male_____

3. Head of the household:

myself_____ spouse_____ father_____ mother_____ grandparent_____ other_____

4. Your annual family income:

under $10,000_____ $10,000 to 19,999_____

$20,000 to 25,000_____ $26,000 or more_____

5. Place of birth: Puerto Rico__ United States__ Other__

6. If born in Puerto Rico, have you lived outside of Puerto Rico for more than three consecutive months?

Yes__ No__ Where?_____

7. If born in the United States, have you lived outside the United States for more than three consecutive months?
Yes___ No___ Where?_____

8. What is your high school general academic average (GPA)?
     4.00–3.50   _____
     3.49–2.50   _____
     2.49–1.50   _____
     1.49–.80   _____
     Graduated with the General Equivalency Diploma_____

9. College credits successfully taken:
     1–15_____   31–45_____
     16–30_____   46–65_____

10. Father's place of birth:
Puerto Rico___ United States___ Other_____
City or Town_____

11. Father's occupation: _____

12. Father's education:
     a. Elementary school_____   b. Middle school___
     c. Secondary school___   d. College or university_____
     e. None_____

13. Mother's place of birth:
Puerto Rico___ United States_____ Other_____
City or Town_____

14. Mother's occupation:_____

15. Mother's education:
     a. Elementary school___   b. Middle school___
     c. Secondary school___   d. College or university___
     e. None___

16. Did both of your parents rear you? Yes_____ No_____

17. If you answered no to question no. 16, indicate which parent, if applicable, raised you:
mother____ father____ other_____

18. If someone else (guardian) raised you, what was the relationship of the person(s) to you? (grandmother, uncle, etc.)_____

19. Guardian's place of birth:
Puerto Rico_____ United States____ Other_____
City or Town_____

20. Guardian's occupation: _____

21. Guardian's education:
      a. Elementary school_____   b. Middle school___
      c. Secondary school_____   d. College or university____
      e. None____

22. Language(s) spoken at home: _____
_____

CUESTIONARIO

(Versión en Español)

Instrucciones: Favor llenar el siguiente cuestionario cuidadosamente. Es importante que usted provea la información requerida.

1. Nombre: _____

2. Edad: 17–21_____ 22–26_____ 27–30_____ 31 ó mayor_____

3. Género: femenino_____ masculino_____

4. Sostenedor(a) económico de su hogar:
yo mismo(a)_____ esposo(a)_____ padre_____ madre_____
abuelo(a)_____ otro(a)_____

5. Ingreso anual de su familia:
menos de $10,000_____ $10,000 a 19,999_____
$20,000 a 25,000_____ $26,000 o más_____

6. Lugar de nacimiento: Puerto Rico_____ Estados Unidos_____

7. Si nació en Puerto Rico, ¿ha vivido usted por más de tres meses consecutivos fuera de Puerto Rico?
Si_____ No_____ Dónde?_____

8. Si nació en Estado Unidos, ¿ha vivido usted por más de tres meses consecutivos fuera de Estados Unidos?
Si_____ No_____ Dónde?_____

9. ¿Cúal fue su promedio general académico de escuela secundaria (superior)?

        4.00–3.50   _____

        349–2.50   _____

        2.49–1.50   _____

        1.49–.80   _____

        Me gradué con el Diploma General Equivalente_____

10. Créditos universitarios aprobados:

        1–15_____   31–45_____

        16–30_____   46–65_____

11. Lugar de nacimiento del padre:

Puerto Rico_____ Estados Unidos_____Otro País_____

Pueblo ó Barrio_____

Comunidad_____

12. Ocupación del padre: _____

13. Educación del padre:

        a. Escuela elemental____   b. Escuela intermedia____

        c. Escuela secundaria____   d. Colegio ó universidad____

        e. Otra_____

14. Lugar de nacimiento de la madre:

Puerto Rico_____ Estados Unidos_____ Otro país_____

Pueblo ó Barrio_____

Comunidad_____

15. Ocupación de la madre: _____

16. Educación de la madre:

        a. Escuela elemental____   b. escuela intermedia___

        c. escuela secundaria_____   d. Colegio ó universidad____

        otra_____

17. Fué su crianza con ambos padres? Sí_____ No_____

18. Sí no se crió con ambos padres, con quién se crió?
madre_____ padre_____ otra(o)_____ guardián_____ otro_____

19. Con qué parientes como abuela(o) tía(o) ó guardian se crió_____?

20. Pariente(s) o guardian(es) lugar de nacimiento:
Puerto Rico_____ Estados Unidos_____ Otro país_____
Pueblo_____
Barrio_____ Comunidad_____.

21. Nivel de educación de parientes o guardian(es):
      a. Escuela elemental_____   b. Escuela intermedia_____
      c. Escuela secundaria_____   d. colegio ó universidad_____.

22. Ocupación de pariente(s) ó guardian(es):_____
Idioma(s) hablado(s) en tú hogar:
_____

REFERENCES

Atkinson, J. W. 1964. *An introduction to motivation.* Princeton, NJ: Van Nostrand.

Atkinson, J., and N. Feather, eds. 1966. *A theory of achievement motivation.* New York: Wiley.

Blalock, H. Jr. 1979. *Social statistics.* 2nd ed. New York: McGraw-Hill.

Blane, H. T., and K. Yamamoto. 1978. Sexual role identity among Japanese and Japanese-American high school students. *Journal of Cross-Cultural Psychology.*

Bonilla, F., and H. Colon. 1979. Puerto Rican return migration in the 1970s. *Migration Today* (April).

Brameld, T. 1958. Explicit and implicit culture in Puerto Rico: A case study in educational anthropology. *Harvard Education Review.*

Calhoun, E. E. 1975. Value orientations of Mexican-American and Anglo-American ninth grade students. PhD diss., New Mexico State University.

Carter, R. E. 1956. An experiment in value measurement. *American Sociological Review* 21 (April):156–63.

Castañeda, A. 1973. Cultural democracy in education. In G. Nimnicht and J. Johnson, eds. *Beyond "compensatory education."* San Francisco: Far West Laboratory.

Castañeda, A., T. Gray, and R. Garcia. 1973. Bicultural achievement motivation scale. Stanford University.

Castañeda, A. and T. Gray. 1974. Bicognitive development and bilingual bicultural education. *Educational Leadership.*

Caudhill, W. and G. DeVos. 1956. Achievement, culture and personality: The case of the Japanese Americans. *The American Anthropologist.*

Caudill, W. and H. Scarr. 1962. Japanese value orientations and culture change. *Ethnology.*

Chen, G. M. 1988. A comparative study of value orientations of Chinese and American families: A communication view. EDRAS.

Child, E. L. 1943. *The second generation in conflict: Italian or American?* New Haven: Yale University Press.

Child, I., T. Storm, and J. Veroff. 1958. Achievement themes in folktales related to socialization practice. In *Motives in fantasy, action and society,* ed. J. Atkinson. Princeton. Van Nostrand.

Christensen, E. W. 1975. Counseling Puerto Rican—some cultural considerations. *Personnel and Guidance Journal.*

Clark, C. 1957. *The conditions of economic progress.* 3rd ed. London: McMillan.

Clissold, S. 1966. *Latin-America: A cultural outline.* New York: Harper & Row.

Cohen, R. A. 1969. Conceptual styles, culture conflict and nonverbal tests of intelligence. *American Anthropologist.*

Coleman, J., 1966. *Equality of educational opportunity*. Washington DC: U.S. Department of Health, Education and Welfare.

Cordasco, F., and E. Bucchioni. 1972. *The Puerto Rican community and its children on the mainland*. Metuchen, New Jersey: Scarecrow Press.

Cortés, C. 1974. Revising the "all American soul course": A bicultural avenue to educational reform. In *Mexican Americans and educational change*, A Castañeda, M. Ramírez III, (Eds.) New York: Arno Press.

Cooper, P., ed. 1972. *Growing up Puerto Rican*. New York: Arbor House.

DeCintron, C. 1975. *Social dynamics of return migration to Puerto Rico*. Río Piedras, Puerto Rico: Social Science Research Center.

Dempsey, T. M. 1973. Variations in value orientations as four subgroups of migratory agricultural workers. PhD diss., University of Miami.

Deutsch, M. 1967. Minority groups and class status as related to social and personality factors in scholastic achievement. *The Disadvantaged child*. New York University.

Devereux, G., and E. M. Loeb. 1943. Antagonistic acculturation. *American Sociological Review*.

De Vos, G.1968. Achievement and innovation in culture and personality. In The study of personality: An interdisciplinary approach, ed. E. Norbeck, D. Price-Williams,

_____. 1965. Achievement orientation, social self-identity and Japanese economic growth. *Asian Survey*.

Díaz-Royo, A. 1975. The enculturation process of Puerto Rican highland children. PhD diss., State University of New York at Albany.

Dinnerstein, L., and Reimers, D. 1975. *Ethnic Americans: A history of immigration and assimilation.* New York: Harper & Row.

Doob, L. W. 1960. *Becoming more civilized: A psychological exploration.* New Haven, Conn.: Yale University Press.

DuBois, C. 1955. The dominant value profile of American culture. *American Anthropologist.*

Eastman, C. E. 1971. Cultural value orientations of Spanish Americans and Anglo-Americans in New Mexico. PhD diss., Cornell University.

Echevarría-Hernández. 1976. Desarrollo del concepto deidentidad en la cultura puertorriqueña. PhD diss., University of Illinois, Urbana.

Eisenstadt, S. N. 1955. The absorption of immigrants. Glencoe, Illinois: The Free Press.

Ennis, C. D. 1992. Educational value orientations as a theoretical framework for experienced urban teachers' curricular decision making. *Journal of Research and Development in Education.*

Epstein, E. H. 1977. Politics and education in Puerto Rico: A documentary survey of the language issue. Metuchen, New Jersey: Scarecrow Press.

Erikson, E. H. 1965. Childhood and society. New York: Norton & Co.

Erikson, E. H. 1965._Identity, youth and crisis. New York: W. W. Norton & Co.

Fallding, H. 1965. A proposal for the empirical study of values. American Sociological Review (April).

Feather, N. T., and G. Wasyluk. 1973. Subjective assimilation among Ukranian migrants: Value similarity and parent-child differences. Australian and New Zealand Journal of Sociology.

Feather, N. T. 1973. Value change among university students. Australian Journal of Psychology.

Femminella, F. X. 1973. The immigrant and the melting pot. In *Perspective on Urban America*, ed. M. Vrofsky. New York: Doubleday.

Field, W. F. 1951. The effects of thematic apperception on certain experimentally aroused needs. PhD diss., University of Maryland.

Findling, J. 1971. Code and message in bilingual achievement motivation. PhD diss., Yeshiva University.

Fishman, J. A. 1966. Language loyalty in the United States. The Hague: Mouton.

Fishman, J., R. Cooper, and R. Ma. 1971. *Bilingualism in the barrio*. Hague: Mouton.

Fitzpatrick, J. P. 1971. Puerto Rican-Americans: The meaning of migration to the mainland. Englewood Cliffs: Prentice-Hall.

Flores, Juan. 1993 Divided Borders, Essays on Puerto Rican Identity. Houston, Texas, Arte Publico Press.

Foucault, Michel, 1988. The Ethic of Care for the Self as a Practice of Freedom, in the Final Foucault, eds. J. Bernauer and D. Rasmussen. Cambridge, MIT Press.

French, E. G. 1958. Effects of the interaction of motivation and feedback on task performance. In *Motives in fantasy, action, and society*, ed. J. Atkinson. Princeton: Van Nostrand.

———, and G. S. Lesser. 1964. Some characteristics of the achievement motive in women. *Journal of Abnormal and Social Psychology*.

Fromm, E. 1941. *Escape from freedom*. New York: Rinehart & Co.

Gallimore, R. 1969. Variations in the motivational antecedent of achievement among Hawaii's ethnic groups. Paper presentation at Conference on Culture and Mental Health in Asia and the Pacific, University of Hawaii.

Gallo, P. 1974. *Ethnic alienation: The Italian-Americans.* Rutherford, NJ: Fairleigh Dickenson University Press.

Gardner, H. 1983. *Frame of mind: The theory of multiple intelligences.* New York Basic.

Geertz, C. 1973. *The interpretation of cultures.* New York: Basic Books.

Gillin, J. 1955. Ethos components in modern Latin-American culture. *American Anthropologist.*

Ginorio, A. B. 1979. A comparison of Puerto Ricans in New York with native Puerto Ricans and Native Americans on two measures of acculturation: Gender role and racial identification. PhD diss., Fordham University.

Glantz, O. 1978. Native sons and immigrants: Some beliefs and values of American born and West Indian Blacks at Brooklyn College. *Ethnicity.*

Glazer, N., and D. P. Moynihan. 1963. *Beyond the melting pot.* Cambridge: MIT Press.

Goldschmidt, W. 1960. The comparative study of values. Exploring ways of mankind (Ed). New York: Holt, Rinehart and Winston.

Gómez-Peña G. 1988. The Multicultural Paradigm, Opening the American Mind,eds. R. Simonson and S. Walker. MN. Graywolf Press.

Gómez Tejera, C., and D. Cruz López. 1970. La escuela puertorriqueña. Troutman Press.

Goodenough, W. 1976. Multiculturatism as the normal human experience. *Anthropology and Education Quarterly.*

Gordon, M. 1978. *Human nature class and ethnicity.* New York: Oxford University, Press.

Gorsuch, R. L. 1969. Rokeach's approach to value systems and social compassion. *Review of Religious Research.*

Gough, H. G. 1957. California Psychological Inventory Consulting Psychologists Press Inc., Palo Alto, California.

Gray, T. C. 1975. A bicultural approach to the issue of achievement motivation. PhD diss., Stanford University.

Greeley, A. M. 1974. *Ethnicity in the United States: A preliminary reconnaissance.* New York: Wiley.

Greer, C. 1974. *Divided society: The ethnic experience in America.* New York: Basic Books.

Grove, C. L. 1974. *The cross-cultural problems of immigrant Portuguese students in American schools.* New York: Teacher's College Institute for Urban and Minority Education.

Gurin, P. and D. Katz. 1966. Motivation and aspiration in the Negro college. Final report, U.S. Department of Health, Education, and Welfare, 1966.

Guthrie, G., and P. J. Jacobs. 1966. Child rearing and personality development in the Philippines. University Park, Pennsylvania State of University Press.

Hallowell, A. I. 1955. *Culture and experience.* Philadelphia: University of Pennsylvania Press.

Hamburger, M. 1958. Realism and consistency in early adolescent aspirations and expectations. PhD diss., Columbia University.

Handlin, O. 1959. *The newcomers.* Cambridge, Massachusetts: Harvard University Press.

Hansen, M. L. 1940. *The immigrant in American history.* Cambridge, Massachusetts: Harvard University Press.

Hauser, R. M. 1972. *Socioeconomic background and educational performance.* Washington DC: American Sociological Association.

Heller, C. 1966. *Mexican American youth: Forgotten youth at the crossroads.* New York: Random House.

Hernández Alvarez, J. 1967. *Return migration to Puerto Rico.* Berkeley: University of California Press.

_____. 1968. Migration, return and development in Puerto Rico. *Economic Development and Cultural Change.*

Hernández Cruz, V. 1973. *Mainland.* New York: Random House.

Hollen, C. C. 1967. *The stability of values and value systems.* MA thesis, Michigan State University.

Horner, M. 1968. Sex differences in achievement motivation and performance in competitive and noncompetitive situations. PhD diss., University of Michigan.

Hull, C. L. 1943. *Principles of behavior.* New York: Appleton-Century-Crofts.

Kagan, S., and M. C. Madisen. 1971. Cooperation and competition of Mexican, Mexican American, and Anglo American children of two ages under four instructional sets. *Developmental Psychology.*

Kantrowitz, N. 1968. Social mobility of Puerto Ricans: Education, occupation and income changes among children of migrants, New York 1950–1960. *International Migration Review.*

Kiley, M. A., and K. A. King. 1992. Differing values of "at-risk" middle school students. American Educational Research Association, San Francisco, California.

Kluckhohn, F. 1953. Dominant and variant value orientations. In *Personality in nature, society and culture*, ed. C. Kluckhohn. 2nd ed. New York: Alfred A. Knopf.

Kluckhohn, F., and F. Strodtbeck. 1961. *Variations in value orientations.* New York: Row, Peterson & Co.

Kroeber, A. L., and T. Parsons. 1958. The concepts of culture and social system. *American Sociological Review* (October).

Kubany, E. S. R. Gallimore, and J. Buell. 1969. Achievement-oriented behavior among Filipinos Living in Hawaii. Unpublished manuscript.

Laguerre, E. A. 1975. Sobre la identidad cultural puertorriqueña. *Revista Interamericana.*

Lahr, D. G. 1968. Time and man-nature value orientations as related to sex identity, ethnic identity and socioeconomic status and as predictors ofacademic success. PhD diss., University of Southern California.

Lambert, W. 1972. *Language, psychology and culture.* Stanford: Stanford University Press.

Lasker, H. 1966. Factors affecting responses to achievement motivation training in India. Honors thesis, Harvard University.

Leavitt, R. R. 1974. *The Puerto Ricans: Culture change and language deviance.* Tucson: University of Arizona Press.

Lehmann, I. J. 1962. Some sociocultural differences in attitudes and values. *Journal of Educational Sociology* (September).

Lesser, G. S., R. Krawitz, and R. Packard. 1963. Experimental arousal of achievement motivation in adolescent girls. *Journal of Abnormal and Social Psychology.*

Lewis, G. K. 1964. *Puerto Rico: Freedom and power in the Caribbean.* New York: Monthly-view Press.

Lewis, O. 1965. *La vida.* New York: Vintage.

Lieberson, S. 1961. A societal theory of race and ethnic relations. *American Sociological Review.*

Lipset, S. M. 1967. The unchanging American character. In *Individualism and conformity in American character*, ed. L. Rapson. Lexington, Massachusetts: D. C. Heath.

Lowell, E. L. 1960. A methodological study of projectively measured achievement motivation. Master's thesis, Wesleyan University.

Macisco, J. J. Jr. 1968. Assimilation of Puerto Ricans on the mainland: A socio-demographic approach. *International Migration Review* (Spring).

Madsen, M. C. 1967. Cooperation and competitive motivation of children in three Mexican subcultures. *Psychological Reports.*

Maehr C. 1974 Culture and achievement motivation. *American Psychologist.*

Maldonado-Denis, M. 1972. *Puerto Rico: A sociohistoric interpretation.* New York: Vintage Books.

_____. 1976. Puerto Rico y Estados Unidos: emigración y colonialismo. Mexico City: Siglo Veintiuno editoriales.

Marjoribanks, K. 1979. Ethnic class, the achievement syndrome, and children's cognitive performance. *Journal of Educational Research*.

McClelland, D. C., J. W. Atkinson, R. A. Clark, and E. L. Lowell. 1963. *The achievement motive*. New York: Appleton-Century.

McKee, J., and A. Sheriffs. 1959. Men's and women's beliefs, ideals and self-concepts. <u>American Journal of Sociology</u>.

Mohr, N. 1977. *In Nueva York*. New York: Dial Press.
Morris, C. W. 1956. *Varieties of human values*. Chicago: University of Chicago Press.

Moss, H. A., and J. Kagan. 1961. Stability of achievement and recognition seeking behaviors from early childhood through adulthood. *Journal of Abnormal and Social Psychology*.

Murray, H. A. 1953. *Thematic apperception test manual*. Cambridge Harvard University Press.

Nahirny, V., and J. A. Fishman. 1965. American immigrant groups: Ethnic identification and the problem of generations. *Sociological Review*.

Nakano-Fultz, J. 1966. A study of status systems and related value orientations among adolescents off an ethnically plural high school community in Hawaii. PhD diss., New York University.

Negrón de Montilla, A. 1971. *Americanization in Puerto Rico and the public school system: 1900–1930*. Río Piedras, Puerto Rico: Editorial Edil.

Nie, N. H. 1975. *SPSS: Statistical package for the social sciences*. 2nd ed. New York: McGraw-Hill.

Nieves-Falcón, L. 1975. *Los emigrantes Puertorriqueños.* Río Piedras, Puerto Rico: Edil.

O'Flannery, E. 1972. Social and cultural assimilation. In *The Puerto Rican community and its children,* ed. F. Cordasco and E. Bucchioni. New Jersey: Scarecrow Press.

Osgood, C. E., J. Suci, and P. H. Tannenbaum. 1978. *The measurement of meaning.* Urbana: University of Illinois Press.

Park, J. S. 1975. A three generational study: traditional Korean value systems and psychological adjustment of Korean immigrants in Los Angeles. PhD diss., University of Southern California.

Parker, S. 1962. Motives in Eskimos and Ojibwa mythology. *Ethnology.*

Parsons, T. 1951. *Toward a general theory of action.* Cambridge, Massachusetts: Harvard University Press.

Patka, F. 1964. *Value and existence.* New York: Philosophical Library.

Pedersen, H. A. 1950. The emerging culture concept: An approach to the study of culture change. *Social Forces.*

Penner, L. A. 1977. A comparison of American and Vietnamese value systems. *Journal Social Psychology.*

Peterson, B., and M. Ramírez. 1971. Illinois. Peal ideal self disparity in Negro and Mexican American children. *Psychology.*

Pettigrew, L. 1964. *A profile of the Negro American.* Princeton: D. W. Nostrand Company.

Pietri, P. 1973. *Puerto Rican obituary.* New York: Monthly Review Press.

Portes, A., R. N. Parker, and J. A. Cobas. 1980. Assimilation or consciousness: perceptions of United States society among recent Latin-American immigrants to the United States. *Social Forces* (September).

Ramírez, M. and A. Castañeda. *Cultural democracy, bicognitive development and education.* New York: Academic Press.

Ramírez, M., and D. R. Price-Williams. 1974. Achievement motivation in Mexican American children. Unpublished manuscript.

Rokeach, M. 1973. *The nature of human values.* New York: The Free Press.
1967. *Value survey.* Sunnyvale, California: Halgren Tests.

Rosen, B. C. 1959. Race, ethnicity, and the achievement syndrome. *American Sociological Review.*

Rosen, B. C., and R. G. D'Andrade. 1959. The psychosocial origins of achievement motivation. *Sociometry.*

Schermerhorn, R. A. 1970. *Comparative ethnic relations: a framework for theory and research.* New York: Random House.

Seda-Bonilla, E. 1967. Social structure and race relations. *Social Forces.*

_____. 1974. Requiem para una cultura. Río Piedras: Ediciones Bayoan.

Seidner, S. S. 1976. *In quest of cultural identity: An inquiry for-the Polish community.* New York: Teacher's College Institute for Urban Minority Education.

Senior, C. 1961. *The Puerto Ricans: Strangers—then neighbors.* Chicago: Quadrangle Books.

Simoes, A. 1976. *The bilingual child.* New York: Academic Press.

Sjostrom, B. 1983. *An analysis of value-orientations of mainland and island Puerto Ricans and non-Puerto Ricans college students*. PhD diss., State University of New York at Albany.

Smith, L. T. 1970. *Studies of Latin-American societies*. Garden City: Doubleday.

Steiner, S. 1975. *The Islands*. New York: Harper Cokophon Books.

Stewart, E. C. 1972. *American culture patterns: A cross-cultural perspective*. LaGrange Park, Illinois: Intercultural Network Inc..

Stockton, W. 1978. Puerto Rican Return Migration. *New York Times* (November 12).

_____. 1984. Puerto Rico: a divided dream. *New York Times* (November 4).

Thomas, P. 1967. *Down these mean streets*. New York: Knopf.

Tirayakian, E. A. 1967. *Sociological theory, values, and sociocultural behaviors*. New York: The Free Press of Glencoe.

Ulibarri, H. 1969. *The Spanish-Americans: A study of acculturation*. Albuquerque, New Mexico: University of New Mexico Press.

U.S. Commission on Civil Rights. 1976. Puerto Ricans in the Continental United States: an uncertain future (October).

Vázquez, F. O. 1979. La socialización formal del estudiante de escuela superior: congruencias-incongruencias de orientaciones valorativas. Revista de   Ciencias Sociales, Centro de Investigaciones Sociales, Universidad de Puerto Rico.

Veroff, Joseph. 1969. Social comparison and the development of achievement motivation. In *Achievement related motives in children*, ed. Charles Smith. New York: Russell Sage Foundation.

Veroff, J., S. Wilcox, and J. W. Atkinson. 1953. The achievement motive in high school and college age women. *Journal of Abnormal and Social Psychology.*

Wagley, C. 1968. *The Latin-American tradition: essays on the unity and diversity of Latin-American culture.* New York: Columbia University Press.

Wakil S. P., C. M. Siddique, and F. A. Wakil. 1981. Between two cultures: A study in the socialization of children of immigrants. *Journal of Marriage and Family* (November).

Weber, M. 1958. *The Protestant ethic and the spirit of capitalism.* New York: Scribner.

Wheeler, T. C. 1972. *The immigrant experience: the anguish of becoming American.* New York: Dial Press.

Whiting, B., ed. 1963. *Child rearing in six cultures.* New York: John Wiley & Sons Inc.

Williams, R. M. Jr. 1960. *American society: A sociological interpretation.* New York: A. A. Knopf.

Williams, R. M. Jr. and E. Sills, eds. 1968. *International encyclopedia of the social sciences.* New York: MacMillan.

Winterbottom, M. 1958. The relation of need achievement to experiences in independence and mastery. In *Motives in fantasy, action, and society,* ed J. W. Atkinson. Princeton: Van Nostrand.

Woodruff, A. D. 1942. Personal values and the direction of behavior. *School Review* 50:32–42.

Woods, F. J. 1956. *Cultural values of American ethnic groups.* New York: Harper and Brothers.

Wurzel, J. S. 1979. A comparative study of the value orientations and individual characteristics of Puerto Rican and Anglo American school children. PhD diss.,Boston University.

Yin, R. K. 1972. *Racial and ethnic identities in American society.* California: Rand & Corp.